Real Stories. Real Strategies.

WOMEN LIKE US
Together Changing the World

Linda Rendleman, MS

ALL PROCEEDS FROM THIS BOOK FUND WOMEN'S LEADERSHIP
THROUGH THE WOMEN LIKE US FOUNDATION.

Published & distributed by:
Linda Rendleman

in association with:
IBJ Book Publishing, LLC.
41 E. Washington St., Suite 200
Indianapolis, IN 46204
www.ibjbp.com

Copyright © 2017 by Linda Rendleman
ALL RIGHTS RESERVED. No part of this book may be reproduced in any manner without the express written consent of Linda Rendleman.

On the cover:
Photo of Naipanoi Kiyonko & Catt Sadler in Kenya, by Melinda DiMauro

ISBN 978-1-939550-53-8

Library of Congress Control Number: 2017930068

First Edition

Printed in the United States of America

DEDICATION

This book is dedicated to the loves of my life
and our next generation:
Jake, Lily, Austin, Arion, Anthony, Alex

ACKNOWLEDGMENTS

Thank you to my daughter Catt who lends her strong voice and her tender heart to our vision for helping women change the world.

Thank you to all the beautiful women who shared their stories of strength, perseverance and love for humanity in this book.
I am grateful.

A very special thank you to Sommer Bannan, writer and educator, who helped me organize this book, communicate with our writers and cheer me on through this process.

Another very special thank you to Jim Cahill, who has lived and breathed this book with me, along with the two previous ones. Thank you for listening and simply being with me on this journey.

Thank you to the following:

Liberty Hill Foundation

Women Connect4Good, Inc., A Foundation

Raven + Lily Ethical Fashion and Lifestyle Brand

Collette Foundation

The CattWalk

Marc Fisher Footwear

Shady Face, Inc.

Claire McDonald, Humanitarian

Melinda DiMauro, Professional Photographer

Shannon Stoddard, Writer

Beads of Esiteti

Sommer Bannan, Educator, Free Lance Writer and Project Manager

Elaine Voci Life Coaching

Kathrin Nicholson, Director of Residential Estates, The Agency Innovating with integrity, collaboration, philanthropy & passion

Karen Caprino-Burg, Founder and Owner, We are Changing Lives; Founder and Publisher, *Indy Metro Woman*

Naiponoi Kiyoko

Vijay Patel

Deanna Schleeter

FOREWORD

I met Linda Rendleman and a group of travelers at Rusinga Island Lodge in Kenya. It was a quick overnight stop for myself and my husband, Raila. The lodge was full, yet they doubled up to make room for us. The group had traveled there from the United States to support women who are making a difference in the lives of children in Kenya. But I didn't know that at first. I didn't know it until I walked through the dining room and saw them sitting in the dim light, each sipping a glass of wine, and discussing their day with the children they had come to help. One of the women asked me to join them. I said "why not."

It was then that I learned about the work of Women Like Us Foundation and the passion these women have for supporting women's leadership for world change. It was then that I learned that these women were in Kenya to also make a documentary film that would shed light on the power of women to make a difference, with a call to action for the viewer to do the same. And it was then that I learned that they, and I, are of like mind and purpose for lifting up the work of women through compassion, communication and collaboration for all humanity.

We shared our passions that evening. And I had the opportunity to share with them the work I have done in Kenya to move forward the power of women in all areas: education, economics and human rights.

It was only one evening. One important evening when two worlds collided, however brief, yet found unity of purpose.

I accepted their offer to be in their documentary and was able to be interviewed for their film by the journalist who was in their group, Catt Sadler. It was my opportunity to tell others what I have done and plan to do to improve women's lives in my country. And as we talked, we knew we were of the same understanding and passions.

It is my honor to write the foreword for this important book that sheds light not only on issues that are important to gender equality and social justice, but also the strong and beautiful souls of women whom, among many, are leading the way for change and empowerment.

When you read Linda's personal stories, you'll understand her vision and how she has become the humanitarian and champion of women that she is. And when you read the women's stories, you'll be motivated and inspired to be among them, find your own path and join all of us: the women of Kenya, the women of America, the women of the world.

-Ida Odinga, Former First Lady of Kenya

TABLE OF CONTENTS

Preface xi
Women Like Us Foundation xiii
Introduction: Catt Sadler xv
Section 1: Women's Leadership 1
    Dianne Hudson: Life is a Flow 11
    Nancy O'Reilly: The Story Behind My Drive to Empower Women 19
    Rachel Roy: If You Put Enough Steps Together, Change Happens 27
    Patricia Darquea: The Woman I Am Today 33
    Sally Colón-Petree: From the Streets of Chicago to a Filmmaker 41
Section 2: Sex Trafficking 48
    Linda Smith: Changing State Law—Helping the Victims 57
    Kyla Smith: Love and Courage for a Better World 65
    K.D. Roche: Why Didn't You Tell Someone? 73
    Jessica Evans: Purchased 77
    Shaunestte Terrell: What These Girls Want is Love 83
Section 3: Homelessness 89
    Lolly Galvin: Sit Next to Someone That Others Walk By ... 99
    Shaaron Funderburk: I Am a Survivor 107
    Caroline Barnett: The Hunger of Homelessness 117
    Marie Griffin: Santa Knows Where You Are Sleeping 127
Section 4: Education 133
    Celeste Mergens: I Am More Than Where I Live 145
    Deb Myers: Preying on Innocence 155

Elissa Kravetz: Radical Self-Acceptance. Kindness. This Is How the World Will Change and Evolve for the Better..**163**

Laura Henderson: Grow Well, Eat Well, Live Well, Be Well.....**171**

Section 5: Kenya.....**178**

Nancy Noël: For The Love of Kenya.....**185**

Mrs. Tom: A School for the Children.....**195**

Mama Margaret: A Passion for Children in Kibera Slums.....**199**

Ann Kabui: Touching the Lives of Teens in Kenya.....**209**

Beth Mwangi: Empowering Women in Rural Kenya.....**217**

Kim DeWitt: Making a Difference for Victims of Female Genital Mutilation.....**227**

Conclusion.....**233**

Biographies.....**235**

Bibliography.....**263**

About the Author.....**268**

PREFACE

Our November 2016 election offered our first chance to put a woman in the office of President of the United States. We came so close. For half a century, women have fought to bring our energy, our minds and our uniqueness to the forefront of our nation's leadership. We have more work ahead.

My husband says stay away from talking about politics. My friends warn of neutrality as the best course. But I'm not making political statements here. I'm making humanitarian statements. I'm not out to tell anyone how to vote or who to pick for a leader. My message is to tell you to keep on pushing, keep on leading, keep on taking a stand for phenomenal women and their absolutely stellar ability to build a better world.

In the following pages you'll read the stories of phenomenal women—their own strategies, personal struggles and personal triumphs. The women I have been blessed to know and who are contributors in this book have taken strides toward the future of all women's leadership in the world. They've set it down, built it up, gathered the troops and, well, kicked butt and taken names...all on their own terms and in their own way.

As you read, you'll find pieces of my story, too. In and out of these pages, I've shared parts of my life and journey as a young woman, then older, and now, today. You'll find exerpts of my own seeking of understanding of issues that are key to my work with the Women Like Us Foundation that supports women-led initiatives against sex trafficking and homelessness, promoting equality in education in the U.S., and key issues for women and girls in Kenya, our global initiative.

Read it in sections or read it straight through. At the end, I hope you feel inspired, educated, aware and motivated to join women of the world to take charge, to get involved.

-Linda Rendleman

WOMEN LIKE US
FOUNDATION

TOGETHER... HELPING WOMEN CHANGE THE WORLD.

OUR VISION

Women Like Us Foundation envisions an educated world with equality for all individuals and collectively coming together in support of social justice.

OUR MISSION

To promote gender equality and social justice through awareness, funding and volunteering for women-led initiatives fighting sex trafficking, homelessness and promoting education.

HOW WE DO IT

Our mission is accomplished through offering grants to women-led initiatives, Women Like Us documentary, Women Like Us books, Women Like Us educational events, and volunteer opportunities.

OUR IMPACT

Women Like Us Foundation has impacted over 9000 lives in the US and globally from 2009 to 2016.

Contact: info@womenlikeusfoundation.org
www.womenlikeusfoundation.org

Catt Sadler

INTRODUCTION

I was born in 1974 in a small town in southern Indiana, with a population of about 10,000. All 'folks' were white, the majority of them Christian, and although I would grow to love this little slice of the world and call it home, there is a portion of Martinsville's history I'm not particularly proud of. To this day, it's still trying to shed its racist reputation.

As I was growing up I heard stories about KKK rallies in the woods, that the Grand Dragon himself called our community home, and that violence erupted because of this racism. There was a horrific tale about a black woman who came to town selling encyclopedias door to door in the late '60s who was stabbed to death because of the color of her skin. These truths would haunt me as a child. I was instinctively saddened by the thought of what lurked 'yonder.' Lucky for me, my parents were loving, inclusive people who, by example, taught me to love and accept my human brothers and sisters regardless of our differences.

Beyond race, though, my mother (like my late grandmother Freda) is a feminist. I was not only raised to respect other cultures and ideas, but women in my family were always cherished, and valued, and lifted up like any of our male counterparts.

Freda, my mom's mom, was what we would today call a Girl

Boss. And yes, she was even a little bossy. She was sassy and opinionated and incredibly driven. She founded the first-ever female-owned real estate company in Indiana. She and my grandfather then raised three daughters of their own, and you can imagine that this was a house filled with girls with big dreams and big ideas.

These ideals were passed on generation to generation, and although my life began in a small town—literally next door to the one John Mellencamp sang about—I never imagined my journey would encompass the big wide world in the way that it has. I couldn't see it as a little girl. I couldn't predict it. But I think I always dreamt about it subconsciously.

I knew I would get "out," and that there was more. I didn't know what was in store, but there was definitely an itch as I grew older to discover what was outside the confines of Indiana life.

After graduating with a journalism degree from Indiana University and securing my first general-assignment reporting job at a local TV station, I began feeling very unsettled. No one in my entire family or extended family had ever left Martinsville "just because". But in my heart and in my soul, I knew my life's purpose would extend beyond the rolling hills, beautiful foliage and Hoosier hospitality my home had to offer.

Cut to 20 years later and here I am in Los Angeles, now with my own family, and boy has the view changed! I've worked 10 years now for the E! network and have interviewed Johnny Depp, Meryl Streep, Leonardo DiCaprio, Julia Roberts, and Oprah. Oh, and even a first lady: Michelle Obama. It has been hard work, day in and day out, but it has also been ridiculously glamorous, with red carpets, designer gowns, international travels covering the weddings of royals, French film festivals, and Olympic games. I have stamped my passport dozens of times over the years and have, as a result, discovered one of my absolute obsessions: traveling. I am completely infatuated by other cultures, their histories, their architecture, their customs, and their cuisine.

INTRODUCTION

All the while I was raising my two sons and traveling the globe for my job, my mom had been steadily working on developing her foundation, Women Like Us. A cornerstone of her organization has been international travel. She would arrange for large groups of people to travel to an area in need of making change at some level, while also experiencing the richness of these places themselves.

In the summer of 2014, I would go to Kenya for the first time. Mom had planned for herself and a dozen other women to travel to a number of places to do work for the many causes her foundation supports there. At the time, it sounded thrilling, but like so many of us, I didn't have a clue how I was going to leave my kids for nearly two weeks and take time off work, and on top of that, my dad had been diagnosed with stage IV lung cancer. I was resistant to going, but thankfully, my mother knows me well. She said, "Get on the plane." And so I did.

One foot on the ground in Nairobi and I knew I was a long, long way from Martinsville, Indiana. The political unrest in the country at the time was at an all-time high. There were a number of soldiers pacing through the airport with machine guns, and similar armed men greeted us at our first stop, our hotel. Oddly, I wasn't afraid. I was calm and eager to let this adventure unfold as it was intended. After all, this experience was in line with what I had always believed was my destiny in many ways.

In the days to come, I would be changed forever—so much so, it's sometimes hard to find the words.

I would meet Mama Margaret who heads the Tenderfeet School in Kibera, one of the poorest and most dangerous places in Kenya and the largest urban slum in all of Africa. This light, this force of a woman, shared her selfless stories of teaching to dozens of orphans who otherwise wouldn't have an education at all. Many of them were ill, living with HIV. She not only runs a school for them, but takes many of them home and nurtures them around the clock. She was the first angel I would meet.

Then, there were the faces from the Nancy Noël Preschool. This is a school Women Like Us had supported for many years, but it was our first time visiting. I lost my breath, it was so tragic upon first glance. The need, the hunger for human touch. There were hundreds of hungry children who until our visit had never used a paint brush, had never blown through a recorder to make music, had never had their own backpack. Giving to these precious little people would be one of the most rewarding experiences of my life.

In the days to come on Rusinga Island I would meet Mary and her two sons, all three of them diagnosed with HIV. We were filming our documentary and she was brave enough to let us and our cameras into her home. There were mud floors and mosquito nets over pieces of foam on the floor that served as their beds. Mary, somewhat hesitantly and certainly embarrassed, would describe her desperation to earn money to care for her kids. Work was hard to come by and she confessed to selling her body for money, as it was the only way to make ends meet. Her kids needed medication and food and shelter, and after her husband died from AIDS, like so many do, this was her life. I remember hugging them all tightly. I wanted to fix it. Right then and there. I felt hollow and helpless but was grateful to have collided with them on this big planet of ours. I'm rarely speechless, but after that visit I remember feeling silenced.

Less than 24 hours after that I would interview the former first lady of Kenya, as if some miracle dropped out of the sky. She and her husband ascended on the lodge where we were staying, and while our group was gathered around a table in a common area, she walked by and her presence was electric! We persuaded her to have a glass of wine with us where we would learn she was a political powerhouse in Kenya who had dedicated her life to empowering young girls in education and other areas. She agreed to be interviewed by me for our documentary. Her story is incredibly riveting, but also aspirational. Her life's work: to make change for girls and future generations to come.

I had heard the phrase FGM in the news before, and I knew vaguely what it meant, but like so many of us who hear about tragic scenarios over and over again, sometimes we become immune to the true devastation taking place. The Olmalaika Home is a kind of refuge for victims of female genital mutilation. This is where I would meet Jackie and Faith and so many other beautiful, resilient, smart, young women who wanted more for their lives. They often left their families to live in this safe, secure haven after being brutally victimized physically, mentally and emotionally. Kim DeWitt founded this home to give hope to these girls when the culture around them is telling them that their bodies aren't their bodies, their worth is equal to that of a cow, their future isn't their own.

Faith wants to be a doctor. Jackie wants to find her own voice. Walking away from this place, unlike many other places I had encountered thus far, I felt hopeful. Because of one woman, Kim, and her courage to do something, I started to see the possibilities of giving the downtrodden a better life.

In bed at night, I wept…more than once. These people had gotten into my bones and I felt this overwhelming responsibility to combat the atrocities engulfing their lives. To heal them, to restore them, to protect them.

I wanted to give to them because they had given to me. The light….

What I know is that there is poverty everywhere. There is need everywhere, in some form, within a mile of each of our homes. In Martinsville, in Los Angeles, in Africa.

I was touched that my mom asked me to contribute to her book because I am such a believer in our connectedness as humans. I feel strongly that our collective purpose is to work together, regardless of race or origin. That it is our human right—our right as women—to find peace, good health, and education.

I hope you'll read the pages of this book and be inspired.

Perhaps you, too, have the itch but need the nudge like my mom gave me. Go ahead, "get on the plane," literally or metaphorically. You won't regret it.

Section 1 – Women's Leadership

> **"IT'S IN THE REACH OF MY ARMS
> THE SPAN OF MY HIPS,
> THE STRIDE OF MY STEP,
> THE CURL OF MY LIPS.
> I'M A WOMAN
> PHENOMENALLY.
> PHENOMENAL WOMAN,
> THAT'S ME."**
>
> Maya Angelou,
> Phenomenal Woman: Four Poems Celebrating Women

▲▲▲

I think of this book as the gathering of messengers. Each of the stories is from or about women who have made their own way, charged through the obstacles of life and just kept on going. Yet the hearts and souls of women like them, women like us, run deep not only for their own mission in their time but also for sending a message to women everywhere: a message about leadership…a message about struggle…a message about overcoming, getting back up and going for it again…a message about commitment and perseverance.

Yes, our stories are separate to each of us, but the passions are shared. And in the beginning of this book you'll meet some outstanding women who are contributing to a better world for all of us. They've included their stories of struggle and victory, their message of hope and wisdom and have included a message to you, the reader, that is sure to resonate. I hope you are able to connect with their stories on a personal level and in ways the writer may have not even intended. It's through sharing our stories and our strategies from our own lives that we can come together and make a difference in the world. Understanding that we are all one. All Women Like Us.

So whether you were raised on the south side of Chicago in a neighborhood where you were taunted and bullied for being Puerto Rican; or you found your true work with a product that could actually save lives and through it give back to the world; or you lived through the bigotry and anger of the South during the Jim Crow era and bring those lessons with you to be a part of a true movement for women; or you stay true to yourself on your rights of equality and you act on that throughout your life; or you have a thriving designer business that has a passion for giving back to children all over the world; There's no better time for women's leadership than now. It's the time of leaning in, standing up, speaking out, looking forward and doing it together.

For women like us, it's the time of standing strong, linking arms, using our formal educations, or simply the school of hard knocks, and learning the lessons life hands us, then using those lessons to speak up for a better world. And it's the time to bring our sisters along with us in leadership.

We as women can bridge the gap. It's not about us. It's about all of us. Women's leadership is about healing the world. Women's leadership is about standing up for all humanity. It is not about segregation, but rather community. It's about human rights. It's about love and compassion and endurance and kindness. It's about being smart, stepping up, perseverance and possibilities.

It's the time of "leaning in" brought to light most recently through Sheryl Sandberg's book, *Lean In. Women. Work. And the Will to Lead.*

I respect and admire Sheryl Sandberg for writing *Lean In*. She was able to use her position as Facebook CEO and her influences to get the message to millions of women. It's making a difference in how women see themselves in their personal and professional lives. And it's bringing back to the forefront the history of where women have been culturally in the United States. Her book brings to light for many women the possibilities to step up, stand up and speak up. That our leadership is valuable.

Here's an excerpt:

> *From the moment we are born, boys and girls are treated differently. Parents tend to talk to girl babies more than boy babies. Mothers overestimate the crawling ability of their sons and underestimate the crawling ability of their daughters. Reflecting the belief that girls need to be helped more than boys, mothers often spend more time comforting and hugging infant girls and more time watching infant boys play by themselves....*
>
> *Even worse, the messages sent to girls can move beyond encouraging superficial traits and veer into explicitly discouraging leadership. When a girl tries to lead, she is often labeled bossy. Boys ae seldom called bossy because a boy taking the role of a boss does not surprise or offend.*

For women of a certain age, women like me and maybe like you, Sheryl's well-stated points are not unfamiliar. Before Sheryl became one of the leaders who picked up the ball and began running with it again, the earlier generation, my generation, were mentored by Gloria Steinem, Ruth Bader Ginsberg, Oprah Winfrey, Maya Angelou, and others.

I've always been a bit of a restless soul. Writing helps me get my thoughts straight. Putting them down on paper, or more recently on the computer screen, gives me clarity. I wrote an article about a decade ago about feminism. I was praising all the women who had propelled us forward, fought the difficult fight, brought us this far toward believing in and executing our rights. Yet I felt that women got to a comfortable spot and took a break. The women coming up today have many rights and advantages that we didn't have. And because of the National Organization for Women and initiatives like it, plus the dedication of thousands if not millions of men and women advocating to moving the status of women forward, progress has been made.

Almost a decade later, it feels like we're fighting the same battles. Or are we? Here's a piece of my mind from back then.

IS FEMINISM STILL ALIVE?

I consider myself a feminist. I'm for women's rights, women's development, women's advancement in the workplace, and the equality of women! And I think we're still fighting for it.

When I was in college 30 years ago there was lots of talk about feminism. There were the bra-burning days, the demonstrations to get us out of the kitchen and into the workforce, the fight for equal pay, the development of birth control pills, and even the idea of "free" sex.

So where is feminism today? I was reminded recently that women still earn about 75 percent of men's pay, according to the Women's Funding Alliance. I occasionally catch a conversation with some seemingly enlightened male friends who are impressed when a man raises his children on his own. Yet, rarely does the conversation include the same sense of awe when referring to a woman who has raised children on her own.

I think somewhere along the way we stopped being militant. And, I think that's a good thing. Militancy can be destructive. But, I also think we can't forget the cause.

Younger women, those in their 20s and 30s, have always known a world with the acceptance of feminist ideas in it. Their mothers, women like me, perhaps like you, brought the tenets of feminism to them as part of their core values and upbringing. And then there are the young men—young men like my son, who would never believe that any woman should wash his clothes, cook his meals or cater to him. His natural tendencies are for an equal partnership and a relationship of equality and mutual respect with all women.

Many of us have raised our sons with these same core values and they are out in society contributing to a more equal and just world for both sexes. But it seems like we've stopped.

I know it can be argued that the statistics reflecting differences in pay between men and women are still skewed. No one knows exactly what the real difference in pay is, and some argue there is none. But, if indeed we are enlightened and have moved forward enough that this is not an issue, why did the case of Lilly Ledbetter vs. Goodyear Tire and Rubber Company recently appear before the Supreme Court? It was yet another cry for equal pay for women. It is evident that many women still don't earn an equal wage.

This topic of feminism goes so far beyond the issue of a paycheck. In the majority of homes of working couples, the female is still mainly responsible for childcare and domestic chores. Issues such as paternity leaves are still odd concepts on many corporate fronts. Old assumptions of female responsibility still remain. Yes, we've made some strides. We have some laws to protect us. But, many of the same issues of thirty years ago are still out there in the workplace, at home and in our relationships.

You can accept the discrepancies you see, or you can speak out against them. We owe it to our sisters, our daughters, and our daughters' daughters, our sons and the men in our lives, to continue the journey. We need to continue the education, the awareness, the values that bring the important contributions of our femaleness into the awareness and appreciation of our society.

And then we got comfortable. Little girls whose mothers fought for equality grew up and slid more easily into understanding the choices they could have in their lives. Little girls whose mothers came to understand their own rights in the world, were given those rights as if they were always there. Little girls of that time period, now as adult women, never question their own rights to have a credit card, have their own checking account, sit at a bar and order a cocktail, run their own companies, make their own living and stand up and speak out for their own needs.

And the women's movement helped us realize that if it doesn't work…we have the right to fix it. We don't have to stay in abusive marriages. We don't have to pick motherhood over a career. We don't have to work all day and clean up, fix up, take care of the family and the home when we aren't at the office. Not everyone's happiness is on our shoulders.

Our expectations in our relationships are changing. We expect partnerships in our marriages. We expect to have choices in careers, lovers and how we spend our time. It's our own time. We don't need to put ourselves last any more. We put ourselves right up front and in turn, teach our daughters and our sons and the universe that human rights include women's rights.

WHERE WOMEN WERE BEFORE THE EARLY 1970S IN THE U.S.:

Women couldn't get birth control if they were unmarried until 1972.

———

Women couldn't serve on a jury until 1973.

———

Women couldn't get an abortion until 1973.

———

Women couldn't get credit cards in their name until 1973.

———

Women couldn't sue for sexual harassment until 1977.

———

Women couldn't keep their job while pregnant until 1987.

———

Women couldn't refuse to have sex with their spouse until 1993.

———

Women couldn't pay a man's rate for insurance until 2010.

———

Women still aren't paid the same as their male counterparts.

———

Fact: A woman ran for President of the United States for the first time in history. 2016.

A STUDENT, A MOMMY AND THE VIETNAM WAR

The campus was buzzing with tension that day when I was walking to class at Indiana University in the early 1970s. I had started my day like always. Up early to feed my baby daughter Jane. Dropped her off at the babysitter so I could drive the 20 miles to Bloomington to get to my class on time. I had started out living on campus, but after marrying, I lived off campus in our small town some 30 minutes away. But that day, something was different.

Of course, I was aware of the Vietnam War. But I had little time at that point in my life for politics. I was having enough trouble understanding how my own world worked to notice much about how things were working nationally and globally. I walked toward campus, headed toward the Union Building where students would gather, eat, discuss, study. I heard voices. Many voices. Loud voices over a megaphone.

Animated student speakers were shouting to a crowd of thousands…speaking out against the war. The cheering from the crowd was deafening. Opposition had finally reached a tipping point not only at our university but at many others across the country. The activity frightened yet intrigued me. I wanted to be a part. I wanted to simply stop and join these thinkers and changers. I wanted to share in their energy.

But I had to get to class. I knew I needed to get my degree first. It wasn't my time to take part. It wasn't my time to act on what I inherently knew to be my right. I envied those who knew what was right and wrong and could express it so clearly. Crazy, because my major course of study was public speaking—but this little girl from the town down the road was still figuring it out. I think that public speaking degree I eventually earned was in some way preparation for a future of speaking up for women and who I am today. That day, I just didn't know it yet.

So I walked through the protest lines, into Ballantine Hall, and took my seat in my English composition class—another step of preparation toward where my life experiences would take me.

Today, I am proud to share the messages of powerful, beautiful and strong women through their stories, and in turn, share pieces and parts of my own.

▼▼▼

Dianne Hudson is one of those strong women. She lived during troubled times, too. As a young African American woman she always knew her life was going to be special, in spite of the exclusion and harshness she experienced from racial conflict. Today she's had many experiences that have shaped her, including her time with Oprah Winfrey as her Executive Producer. She found herself on the forefront of change for women in America.

Dianne Hudson

LIFE IS A FLOW

> ❝ GET YOURSELF **ALIGNED** WITH THE STUFF THAT'S IN THE BACK OF YOUR MIND AND IS CALLING YOU. ❞

I grew up in a pivotal time in history. I grew up seeing so many changes. I grew up during the Jim Crow laws that forced segregation. And as an African American little girl in South Carolina, I didn't understand about racism and bigotry. We really didn't talk about it much. It was a way of life and all I knew.

I was fortunate. I came from a family with educated parents and grandparents. They were all teachers. We lived in a family environment and it was kind of like a compound. All of our aunts, uncles, and cousins were in the same neighborhood, very nearby. I had lots of love and nurturing and wasn't affected as a child by the turmoil outside my small world.

I went to Catholic school. And, although there was a Catholic school within walking distance, mine, the black school, was across town. We had black nuns, but the priests were white. I have a summertime memory of when I was about seven years old watching kids in the neighborhood walk by our house in swimming suits, carrying towels. I asked my grandmother, "Where are they going?" Grandmother responded, "To the swimming pool, but you're not allowed to go." We just accepted that we had different rules. We were able to go to the beach, but only the "colored" beach. It wasn't as nice as the white beach.

THE BIGOTRY DID AFFECT ME

In hindsight, the bigotry did affect me. At the time, it was the way it was. Rules were you didn't get upset that you couldn't go to the pool. My parents never told me why I couldn't go; they didn't say it was because of the color of our skin. I got lots of "no's" without explanation.

In today's world, white people who didn't live during those times as an African American have an attitude of "Get over it…that is history…don't bring up the race card…things have changed." But experiences have chains.

We eventually moved to Baltimore where my eyes were opened to change happening in the country. Busing became a part of my childhood. I went daily to the suburbs for school. In an effort to integrate the schools, many black children were sent out of their area. The bus rides were long. Many of us felt displaced. When my classmates would have activities and get-togethers after school, I was not included.

I DIDN'T LIVE IN THE NEIGHBORHOOD

There were many critics of busing, and I understand why. But I do understand what they were trying to do. In certain ways, busing opened up a level of exposure for me that may not have happened otherwise. I went to school in a Jewish community and it was my first look at any beliefs outside the Christian religion. I learned social skills that came with meeting people other than what I had always known in my life. Some kids didn't adapt well to the busing experience. It was too foreign. But not me: my world got bigger. I was exposed to a life developing for me.

I'm reminded of the story Oprah tells when her grandmother said, "You better watch to see how I do this clothes washing… so you can do it someday." Oprah remembers thinking, I don't think so.

I KNEW MY LIFE WAS GOING TO BE INTERESTING

I always just kind of knew I was going to be someplace else. And as I grew more and more into adulthood, I felt my life was going to be interesting. I was getting more skills. Success skills, in a way.

I was fortunate to have educated parents. It was a given that I would go to college. I supposed I would get a teaching degree like the rest of my family, but my mother encouraged me to think bigger, to think of what I love and what I was good at, and make it my career. I was a natural writer, so my direction became journalism.

As a kid, we had three TV stations. It was the talk shows like *Merv Griffin* and *Dinah Shore* that I always wanted to watch. While my friends watched *Mickey Mouse Club* or some after-school kids' show, I was fascinated by the talk shows. When I was asked to be a production assistant for a local talk show, I got a glimpse of what I had been preparing for all along. In a field like this, it wasn't like other careers. There were few female mentors and teachers to help lead the way. And not for a black woman, especially.

I got my first taste of affirmative action when I was a senior in college. The Associated Press called me and was looking to hire. I was referred to them by one of my professors. They had a writing test I needed to take, so I did that. Then they gave me the job. I was confused. It was hard to understand how I could get a job simply through a test and with no interview. When I asked them about it, they explained that the reference from my professor was good enough. It dawned on me that they were fulfilling the new affirmative action requirements set forth by the government. It was a way of implementing opportunities for us after the lifelong insidious exclusion that we experienced. Many others didn't understand…many still don't.

EIGHT WOMEN AND OPRAH

What happened for me was I spent 10 years of my career working on local talk shows in Detroit. Then I got a call. There was an African American woman hosting a new show, and she was putting together a team. She was going up against *The Phil Donahue Show* in Chicago. And she was launching the show in 30 days! Right then I knew this was going to be something special. And within two weeks of launch, Phil Donahue was struggling and *The Oprah Winfrey Show* was off and running.

We were an all-woman crew with the opportunity to communicate to women and relate in a different way. It wasn't just news. In fact, news wasn't layered enough for me. This was my opportunity to build depth in stories and experiences that news didn't allow.

I was one of eight who started with Oprah. We did five live shows per week. It wasn't long before it became clear to Oprah that we should build in the spiritual and philanthropic component. No more regular talk-show stuff.

I became Executive Producer and was in charge of ratings. My instructions were to change the show and yet stay number one. It was a challenge. At first, viewers didn't understand the philanthropy or spirituality angles. It was the mid-'90s and there was no differentiation between spirituality and religion like there is today. Spirituality meant church then and that confused some viewers.

But we kept pushing. Oprah would tell me, "Dianne, this isn't just a show…it's a mission." So we developed the Angel Network and began our quest to uplift and inform…to give a broader perspective and open up the world to one another. We developed a Christmas Kindness effort for needy children and put it on the show; we took food and toys to thousands of kids in Africa and put it on the show; we started the school in Africa and asked people to donate on the show. We got on Nelson Mandela's radar. And the rest is history.

And right now, today, when I turn on OWN, I can't even tell you how great it feels for me to watch it. To know that I was a part of that journey and the richness it gave the life of a little black girl from a segregated community in the South, along with the rest of the world.

COOPERATE WITH LIFE

For me, what is important, and my words to others, is to get yourself aligned with the stuff that's in the back of your mind and is calling to you. Don't wait until you get other things in order. Don't be the one who says, "As soon as I get this done, then I will follow my path." Don't wait. Align your passions with those things in your life that matter to you. Is it church, work, family, speaking, writing? Be it the environment, helping the homeless, mentoring younger women…follow whatever may be your direction that fills you up.

When you are sincere and true in your actions, one thing leads to another. Bring a lot of insight and passion to what you want to do. Life is open-ended. Everyday is just the beginning. The path won't end; it will develop into what it should be. It will take its own form when you put energy behind it and it is right for you.

The interesting thing about life is the Big Plan. God's Plan! And if you learn to "cooperate" with the plan, or simply cooperate with the unfolding of your life and recognize it as the intentional plan, match it with your dreams and you have the power to live life in accordance with your purpose.

Don't put things off until you win the lottery. Get in the flow of your life even though you may not have it all lined up perfectly. Just get in there. If you can't make your goals and dreams top priority right now, it's OK, because you don't know how today's experiences are going to serve you down the road.

It's like a little seed. Give it some water…and it grows and thrives.

I'm sure there's lots of stories like mine. So many of us who were tied to the "shoulds" of life and the role we played as women. It never did seem right. There always seemed like there was something more. It was a restlessness. An unanswered question that sat somewhere between our hearts and our brains. Maybe in our throats…until we found our voices.

Dianne Hudson-Producer and Entrepreneur

▲▲▲

Nancy O'Reilly grew up around the same time as me. She knows the struggles of women in those 70s years. And, like me, didn't understand why that should be. So Nancy took her own path, eventually speaking up and out for women's leadership, authoring books, hosting her radio show and creating a foundation for women to connect and do the work of changing the world. She is a philanthropist, a mother, a grandmother and a humanitarian. And she found that being a woman is, indeed, a wonderful thing.

▼▼▼

Nancy O'Reilly
THE STORY BEHIND MY DRIVE TO EMPOWER WOMEN

> "I IGNORED THE COMMENTS AIMED AT LIMITING MY OWN EMPOWERMENT AND **PURSUED MY DREAM** OF FURTHERING MY EDUCATION AND CAREER, LIKE I HOPED MY DAUGHTERS WOULD DO WHEN THEY BECAME WOMEN."

WHAT WAS SO GREAT ABOUT BEING A WOMAN?

I was the most unlikely person to pursue a career empowering women. A classic tomboy growing up, I really didn't get the girl-thing and much preferred playing ball with the boys to doing anything girls were "supposed to do." When I was about to turn 13, my older sister asked me, "Nancy, when are you ever going to be a girl?" I didn't know what she meant, even though I had amazing role models. Both of my grandmothers were in business and one of them owned a jewelry company. My mother was a successful real estate agent in the D.C. area who had her own money and her own voice. She spoke up about things that were important to her.

Even with these powerful women role models, I thought women got the short end of the stick. I wanted more for them and for me. What was so great about being female? I sure had a lot to learn. God has a sense of humor, because my real lessons began when I got married and had children: one daughter after another, three in all, and—so far—six granddaughters.

PURSUING MY DREAM

All of this was happening in the 1960s and 70s during the first feminist movement when a lot of women were finding their voices and speaking out. I set out to make myself a positive role model for my daughters and to show them they could do anything they wanted in life. When I started on my master's degree, I was surprised to find not just lack of support, but real resistance from the women I knew. They said things like, "But what about your family? What will your small children do while you're at school?" I ignored the comments aimed at limiting me and pursued my dream of furthering my education and career, like I hoped my daughters would do someday.

I continued to build that career with my doctorate in clinical psychology and many successful jobs along the way, including starting my own company, O'Reilly Health and Wellness, LLC. I was volunteering as a crisis responder and living a full and enriched life when I neared my 50th birthday and suddenly felt invisible. This was completely new for me. It was crazy! I had a seat at the table: I sat on boards; I had a voice; I was a respected professional. But in my everyday life, I suddenly felt ignored and insignificant.

I reached out to other women to see if they were feeling the same and was startled to learn they were. I undertook a major study, interviewing 1,200 women of all ages, recording their responses and writing and presenting a professional paper about the results. Ultimately this became the WomenSpeak project, with a website to share important information and the book, *Timeless Women Speak: Feeling Youthful at Any Age*.

By now I had built a good team and we focused on the issues that women said were essential to a fulfilling and successful life: relationships, careers, health and fitness and self-esteem. I also reached out with a radio podcast on these subjects and introduced authors and speakers to my WomenSpeak community, sharing their valuable information and supporting their work and their books.

All of these issues began to center around empowerment and helping women find and use their authentic, unique strengths. This process led to my second book, *Leading Women: 20 Influential Women Share Their Secrets to Leadership, Business and Life*, a collection of stories and advice to help women become the leaders they were born to be. It was exciting to have 19 women leaders—selected from hundreds of accomplished podcast guests—accept my invitation to contribute to this book. I was working hard, taking my passion to empower women to the next level, when I got the wake-up call of my life.

OUR GREATEST CHALLENGES PROVIDE OPPORTUNITIES FOR GROWTH AND CHANGE

My marriage of 42 years collapsed. In just a few minutes, my life changed forever. I was devastated. Here I was, urging women to claim their power, be resilient and live their best lives, while my own life was literally falling apart. I realized that my purpose, originally pursued to help my daughters and then other women, had to be applied to myself. I needed to walk the walk, listen to myself and follow my own advice to claim my power. It didn't happen overnight, but it did happen and a new message emerged from its ashes: the importance of women helping women. I wouldn't have been able to survive the trauma without my sisters. My female friends and family members listened, propped me up and urged me forward. Their love and compassion restored my faith in myself and I discovered that the best revenge is to live well and be successful.

Our greatest challenges provide opportunities for growth

and change. It was not easy for me to reach out for help, but the first lesson I learned is that I had to do just that. Like most women, I am a natural collaborator. It's in our nature to reach out and help others. We have to learn that other people need us to allow them to help us. This builds closer, more rewarding relationships.

Next I had to get past my fears, which threatened to drown me when my anchor disappeared. I was adrift and my self-confidence was shaky. Again, my women friends saved me. I not only got past my fears, I set out to do the very things I was afraid of. When I accomplished one of them, I checked it off and went on to the next. Soon I wasn't fearful any more. I proved to myself that I was the only person who could stop me. And guess what: I learned that anchor also held me down. I became more empowered without it.

I said "yes" to opportunities that have led me through an amazing journey. I attended retreats and seminars; I traveled and learned things to help me continue growing. I met new people and made new friends. And I accepted invitations to sit on boards. I now serve as Chairman of the Board of The Statue of Responsibility Foundation, which is developing funds to build a monument on the West Coast to bookend The Statue of Liberty on the East Coast. This monument seeks to engage people in a new movement of responsibility to ensure our freedoms for future generations.

I also began a new love affair. It was both mutual and satisfying. I fell in love with horses, began collecting and riding, then showing and breeding. The warmth and trust that flows between me and my horses not only calms my busy mind, it fills me with the joy and gratitude that comes from closely bonding with an animal through pure unconditional love. I began to support equine therapy, since I had personally experienced amazing benefits from close connections with horses.

My strong faith in a higher power guided me onward, through times of doubt, stress and setbacks. A faith that everything happens for a reason and is unfolding as it should help us survive the challenges and thrive in the aftermath of a life-changing crisis. Through all of this I stayed connected to my passion and purpose.

I founded WomenConnect4Good, Inc., a not-for-profit devoted to empowering women. I have experienced some of the most fantastic connections of my life with people in the organizations my foundation has supported, and working with my amazing "Team Nancy" and my *Leading Women* co-authors. I was already connecting for good, and giving the foundation that name allowed me to connect with more people. I truly believe we are changing the world through women empowerment.

It is wonderful to collaborate with sister organizations that have similar missions. We recently began partnering with Take the Lead Women, seeking to prepare, develop, inspire and propel women to take their fair and equal share of leadership positions across all sectors by 2025. That's 70 years earlier than predictions, based on our past rate of advancement.

Believing that we are all connected, and that when one of us suffers, we all suffer, we also connected with The Convoy of Hope Women's Empowerment Program. This powerful international effort teaches women to run their own businesses, and provides micro-loans and a support group of other women. This enables them to provide food and education for their children and to better the economic status of their entire community.

WOMEN HELPING WOMEN

This amazing journey has taught me what this girl-thing is all about. It's about taking our feminine strengths and applying them to the passions that drive us. These supposed "soft skills" enable women to make today's businesses more profitable, our communities more livable, and our laws more supportive of human needs. These soft skills give today's woman the power she needs to change the world. Together, women helping women are making a difference everywhere they apply their skills. Cooperation, not competition, is the new women's movement, and women like me—and you—are connecting for the good of the world.

                Dr. Nancy O'Reilly-PsyD International Philanthropist - Founder of Women Connect4Good, Inc.

▲▲▲

Rachel Roy is a successful clothing designer and humanitarian. She's built her brand to include not only a strategic business model but also included her intense passion for giving back and supporting women's rights for equality and fairness. I'm so happy to have her contribution here where she tells her personal story of changing her situation by understanding the value of hard work and using her voice to help other women do the same.

▼▼▼

Rachel Roy

IF YOU PUT ENOUGH STEPS TOGETHER, CHANGE HAPPENS

> ❝ I'VE ALWAYS FELT RESPONSIBILITY TO GIVE BACK AND TO **GIVE A VOICE** TO WOMEN AND CHILDREN WHO DO NOT HAVE ONE. ❞

Changing the world. It's a big statement. It's a bold idea. It's an idea that can scare a lot of people because of just how massive it sounds. It's easy to get overwhelmed by the thought of it. Where do I start? Will anyone listen to what I have to say? Can I do it by myself? Can I make an impact? How does one *really* go about changing the world?

TRAVELING HELPS SHAPE US

I grew up with modest resources (some would call it poor) in a small town in Northern California. My father grew up in India. My mother was of Dutch descent. Both knew hard work. Both knew struggle. And, both showed my brother and me the world through traveling. What I have realized as an adult is traveling helped shape us.

Traveling made us become better people and therefore we learned, in part, how to contribute to making the world a better place.

It would have been easy for my parents to keep us sheltered in our little town and just focus on the modesty of our own lives. But, perhaps because both my parents had ties to the world at large, traveling with zero money was something that seemed natural to them. It created a platform for something bigger for my brother and me. We both grew up with the courage and conviction to act—acting on making our situation better, acting on becoming the people and doing the things we believed best for us.

Having little growing up, and seeing people with even less in third-world countries, we understood we had nothing to lose with bravery and everything to gain. Together my brother and I began acting on what we saw wrong with the world and we tried to create solutions, one person at a time. Starting with us. We started by changing our situations through hard work. We worked from the age of 14, first in internships and then on college educations. Even if it felt overwhelming or impossible at times, one step at a time in life was doable.

A FEW COINS CAN MAKE A DIFFERENCE

I visited India at three years old and returned again at 40 years old. The trip was equally hard each time. Seeing the children in the streets and how they live is heartbreaking and feels paralyzing. Can the few coins that you give one child really help? And what about the others? This is where you breathe and remember to act—no matter how small.

I became involved with an organization called Children's Hope India, a foundation that builds schools in the slums that ensure children are being educated, fed, and looked after. It's giving the children a real chance and it's making real change. On my most recent trip to India, I visited one of the schools in a slum. I spent the day with the children, seeing them learn, dance, smile and just be children. It's in those moments that you realize you made a difference by supporting a program like Children's Hope India however you can—with money, spreading the word, or calling all your friends for donations of clothes and supplies. A little can build a lot. And you can contribute, brick by brick.

I've always felt a responsibility to give back and to give a voice to women and children who do not have one. Having my own business has afforded me the opportunities to create programs like Kindness Is Always Fashionable, where we work with third-world artisans to create products to sell on RachelRoy.com and in the stores in which I sell my own product. It's a sustainable way of creating work for these talented women artisans, and their employment helps to create living environments where they can pay for their own rent, escape abuse, and earn the respect of husbands who once treated them as servants.

Employment helps secure better futures for these women, their families and their communities. It's one of my absolute purposes in owning a business, because I am the one in charge, making the decision to help women in the third world when I know that working for larger corporations would never afford me those freedoms. Where it becomes more challenging is when you are not the boss, but you want to have your voice heard. And you want change from that.

USING MY VOICE FOR CHANGE

Through my business relationship with Macy's, I was invited to Haiti with Terry Lundgren, the CEO, and Martha Stewart, to meet with Haitian artists to form a commerce program that brought Haitian artisan goods into the United States for sale. It was directly after the earthquakes and the country was in turmoil. I had read a good deal about the camps they had set up for the displaced people and how they were dangerous places. I saw firsthand how women and girls were not safe; violence and rape were alarmingly commonplace. The issue had weighed heavily on me before the trip and on the airplane ride there. I wanted and needed to help but was unsure how.

We had an audience with the president of Haiti, Mr. Michel Martelly. Pleasantries were exchanged. Hands were shaken. He turned to me and asked if I would come back.

Instead of the expected answer of "Yes, of course," I used my voice. I said I would not come back unless he guaranteed the camps would be as safe for women and children as they had been made safe for me that day I walked through them. He was visibly taken aback. I'm sure my traveling companions were shocked I used the audience with the president in this manner, but when an opportunity presents itself, you take advantage.

I think about that moment quite often. It's been two years since that trip. It still weighs heavily on my mind because I do not think I made the situation better for the women and girls in the tent villages. I so badly wanted to change the situation. I just did not know how.

Your voice is loud. Use it. Plant a seed. Then figure out how to water it. To this day, I still am using my voice for change.

If you want to change the world, start with yourself. It's a constant work in progress. To act is to take a step toward change and betterment. If you put enough steps together, change follows. And then more people follow. And more change follows. And things get better. And you get stronger.

Rachel Roy - Philanthropist and Entrepreneur -
Founder of the Rachel Roy Brand and Founder of
Kindness Is Always Fashionable

▲▲▲

Patricia Darquea eats, sleeps and breathes her determination to succeed. Like Rachel, she's created a successful business and includes philanthropy as part of her business plan. Not because she should, but because it is a part of her as a human being. She shares her "aha moment" story that came to her at a time of darkness. The answers are always there; you just need to open up and see them.

▼▼▼

Patricia Darquea
THE WOMAN I AM TODAY

> ❝ THE LESSON **I AM LIVING** IS THE LESSON I AM TEACHING. ❞

My name is Patricia Darquea. I'm the proud daughter of two wonderful Austrian parents who immigrated to the United States from Vienna. Their American dream was difficult for them to obtain, especially coming from Europe speaking broken English and with only two suitcases in hand. They overcame and conquered their fears, never sacrificing their scruples nor jeopardizing their integrity. I can proudly say that my parents instilled this "fire in my belly" to succeed; they are my examples. My daily reminders and inspiration to persevere developed through the most impossible of circumstances in their search for a better quality of life in America. Coming from nothing and surviving World War II was the hardest obstacle they had to overcome.

MAKING A DIFFERENCE "GREATER PERSON TODAY THAN I WAS YESTERDAY"

Making a difference in this world is a desire. It's an instinct to do something great for mankind. It's a passion one is born with. You eat, sleep, and breathe your determination to succeed. My journey in life began on a path, as a professional public speaker, a spokesperson who represented a multitude of corporations throughout the United States alongside some of the country's most influential executives. As I first began my career, I didn't realize that every step I took or person I met was a building block or link to complete my full circle of who I am today. All encounters, experiences, and people you meet are meant to be within your life and within your destiny. Everyone's path through life is predetermined. What really matters is what you do with your skills, the people you meet and the positive accomplishments you bring along the way through your journey in life.

This voyage that I found myself on as the inventor of the ShadyFace Sunshade brand was actually thrown at me like a life preserver, a curve ball, which happened accidentally to me a few years ago after a near-fatal accident. I realized my life was spared for a reason. That was the year I will never forget.

THE DARKEST DAYS OF MY LIFE. MY DESTINY... MY CHANCE TO SURVIVE

My destiny changed into the darkest days of my life in 2009. I can still remember how great my life was with my husband and family, finally settling back into our daily routine after coming home from a two-month trip to Europe. We were busy traveling overseas for business and pleasure, bringing in the New Year with joy after completing a successful and healthy 2008. I can still remember rejoicing and dancing among all the beautiful long gowns and waltzing throughout the Hofburg Palace in Vienna at the Kaiser Ball. I had no idea that enchanted evening was going to be the last waltz I'd dance for a very, very long time.

The lesson I am living is the lesson I am teaching. Never take anything for granted. Be grateful for all your loved ones in life. Have gratitude when waking up healthy every morning. Acknowledge the blessing in having two eyes to see with, two hands to hug with and two legs to walk the straight line with. We have all been given the gift of life, which we hang onto like a fine string. That string can snap at any time, like what happened to me. One minute I was living such a great life, and then my life came to a radical halt. I will never forget that night in early February that almost took my life. Little did I know that night was going to be the pivotal point of whether I stayed on earth or I said "Goodbye".... Thanks to my guardian angel, I stand strong today.

It's rather difficult to write or even talk about that incident. It was the most horrific encounter my husband and I had ever witnessed or experienced. My husband's words still resonate in my mind when describing my survival after my excruciating fall down a set of stairs: "Most people would not have survived your impact...."

My husband and I were rushing that evening to catch a theatre performance. We were getting ready, quickly scurrying around the house, grabbing a few items to rush out the front door. My last recollection was seeing my husband at the bottom of the staircase, still smiling and complimenting me as we were getting ready to leave for a lovely evening. That night changed my life forever. My destiny was altered as my own high-heel shoe hooked itself into my pant leg.

The next thing I can recall was feeling my soul levitating out of my body as I was lying on the hardwood floor, face down at the bottom of the staircase. I could see myself rising, feel the sensation of lifting, while a calm and comforting sensation overcame me. I know I was leaving the earth into another dimension. My husband's intense screams and cries brought me back. Thank God for my husband. Thank God he was present that night, or I would not be here today.

"I can hear you honey," I whispered in my own head as I came to. He began carefully turning me around and immediately called the ambulance while asking me to hold my upper lip together. Shortly thereafter, I was in the ambulance with the sirens on. The ER team pushed me through the hallways, right into a noisy CAT scan machine. It was around 11:00 p.m. and my husband summoned a plastic surgeon, outside of the hospital's staff that evening, who came to my side shortly before midnight. I should have known that it was a very serious situation when my parents were showing the surgeon my modeling photos; I should have known when no one would show me a mirror. The intense mercy I experienced is hardly describable. A plastic surgeon whom I've never met before came to my aid, as I was being put under anesthesia. My husband and parents were crying and squeezing my hand while I entered the surgical room. This was my destiny, a chance to survive.

Many months went by while I was bed-bound, completely wrapped like a present in gauzes and bandages, with a severe case of vertigo and headaches. As I lay in bed looking out the window, I searched for answers. How was I going to overcome this physical trauma? Why did this happen? Will I work again once my body is healed? How will I get on with my life?

I'm thankful for the guardian angel who helped me survive that fall and impact. I'm thankful the most talented surgeon was sent to my aid; he was given the task of stitching my inner facial muscles and upper vermilion (which had been torn up), so I could smile again. I had given myself a cleft lip and I broke my nose. Three years and four nose surgeries later, and after nine months of healing and recuperating, I am who I am today!

MY GIFT FROM GOD...BONDING, HEALING AND "LICKING OUR WOUNDS" TOGETHER

Within the first few weeks of soul-searching after my accident, I realized I needed a pet. I began looking online for Pomeranian rescue shelters. I knew it was a risk; many animals are in shelters because they are either misplaced or abused.

But I needed to begin my own healing by giving a pet another chance at love and a great home. Soon thereafter I was given a "GFG" (Gift from God) and found Romeo! I quickly named him that because of Valentine's Day. I knew it wasn't going to be easy, since he had been mentally hazed by children and abused by men. This boy went through his own hell and was a survivor! We were perfect for each other. My healing needed this dog and he needed me to rescue him. It's been a love affair ever since… bonding, healing and "licking our wounds" together.

A POSITIVE HEALING RETREAT

Six months later my family decided to do a getaway vacation to Maui, to get me out and change my outlook with a "positive healing retreat." The island was so tranquil and the zen ambiance was great. My stay in our resort offered a lot of time to rest. While watching families interact with one another on the beach, it dawned on me that everyone was in one way or another struggling with the complexity of the intense sun exposure. Tourists and locals were fighting off the heat on the beach, at restaurants, or relaxing by pools. Everyone was using some form of unconventional objects just to protect themselves and their children. This became the vacation that changed my life forever. I thought of my amazing "miracle idea" called ShadyFace!

MY LIFE PASSION AND GIVING BACK

Through my company I'm able to dedicate my life to my true passions. My passion and purpose is to assist and help children with life-threatening illnesses and to help animals that need to be rescued. Through my business endeavors, I'm able to help others who are vulnerable and in need. My ShadyFace Corporation donates ShadyFace Sunshades to the Ronald McDonald auctions and fundraisers. The money raised goes toward medical bills and housing for families so they can be close to their children as they undergo medical treatments. We donate our ShadyPaw Sunshades for auctions and fundraisers to the Humane Society and to numerous "no-kill" shelters. In addition, we support rescue homes that rehabilitate animals from shelters and from the hands of their abusers. Proceeds of ShadyFace Bluetooth Speakers apply to The American Families of Fallen Soldiers and financially assist many women's charities for a better life...for a second chance.

Through my accident and my own healing, I have learned the importance of perseverance, and the value of giving back. Today I walk with my head held high, holding my two rescue dogs tightly in hand, on a solid path into a positive future.

My message to others is to "find a plight, a cause, or a service where your voice and energy can be heard."

Patricia Darquea-Founder of ShadyFace

▲▲▲

Sally Colón-Petree was raised on the south side of Chicago. A Puerto Rican "chick" as she calls it, in an all-white neighborhood. When you read her story, you'll feel a closeness to her and you'll understand that if she can do it, you can, too. Sally's out to change the world through her talent as a filmmaker, her tender heart, and her incredible perseverance.

▼▼▼

Sally Colón-Petree
FROM THE STREETS OF CHICAGO TO A FILMMAKER

> ❝ I'M NOT GOING TO WAIT FOR SOMEONE ELSE TO DO IT, I'M GOING TO **BE THE ONE** WHO DOES IT! ❞

THE BEGINNING

I grew up on the streets of Chicago, one of the most violent cities in the world. I was an outgoing, young Puerto Rican girl in a white neighborhood where discrimination ran rampant.

In 1964, our parents bought our childhood home. They were not prepared for what followed. What my parents didn't know at the time was that they had moved into an "all white" neighborhood where they were not welcome. The stresses of that time of bigotry and prejudice are embedded in my soul.

GOING COLD TURKEY

My sister and I were taken on a long road trip when I was six years old. My parents didn't tell us where we were going, but my sister and I had a hunch we would be gone for a while. I had no idea that this trip was going to separate my sister and me from our parents for almost a year. Our family trip took us to a rehabilitation center, where both of my parents checked in. Before my mom was admitted, she was required to be "clean." At the age of six, I experienced one of my most vivid and difficult memories of my childhood: I watched my mom go "cold turkey" from a heroin addiction. To this day, I don't understand how I was allowed to see that, why my sister and I weren't protected and shielded from that exposure.

While both of my parents were in rehabilitation, my sister and I were sent to a home in Dover, Pennsylvania, for children of drug addicts. We stayed on a farm with a lot of kids and animals. I mostly have good memories of being there. On the farm, the kids would wake in the early mornings to run to the chicken coops to pick out fresh eggs, and in the winter we all had fun tobogganing down the snow-covered hills. Our parents were allowed to visit us once a month. I remember the excitement of getting ready for the visit, putting on my best outfit, the house supervisor curling my hair. I loved my mom and dad so much and as a child I couldn't understand why our family had to be separated.

My mom decided not to go the full term of her rehabilitation. One late night my sister and I were awakened by one of the adults in the home. We were asked to pack our belongings. They took us outside where my mom was waiting for us. We drove away and never returned to that home. After a short distance to the nearest highway, oddly enough, we were dropped off on the side of the freeway, where we hitchhiked to the nearest town. My mom had some friends who let us stay in their home for a short time. One of the ladies in the home made custom Barbie dresses. They taught my sister and me how to make fresh strawberry jelly. I loved being in that home.

COMING BACK HOME

Soon after that we headed back to our home in Chicago, to the old neighborhood. We lived on food stamps. I remember every month my mom would bring home a big block of "government cheese."

For years I tried to make friends, but none of the little girls were allowed to play with "the little Puerto Rican girl from across the street." Every year there was a block party in our neighborhood and we were the only family not invited. My room was at the front of the house, so I remember crying every year as I looked out and saw everyone celebrating and having fun.

This became a harsher reality when I started walking home from school at the age of 10. Almost every day I had two to three bullies waiting for me in the alley, ready to beat me up. In most cases I was able to outrun them, but some days I would come home with bruises on my body and a bloody nose. My mom was working full time as a social worker and was always very tired when she came home after a long day. I didn't tell her what was happening to me. My sister found her escape through a serious relationship, so she was not around much. My grandmother was too busy watching her telenovelas (soap operas) to take much notice.

A few years later my mom met and married a new man, my sister married her long-time boyfriend, and my grandmother passed away. I felt very alone. I began my downward spiral into the land of exploration and rebellion. My first experience was with marijuana. I knew right away that it wasn't for me. Next, I tried alcohol. I was searching to fill the pain and emptiness of my childhood trauma. Eventually I ended up in the home of a much older man who attempted to rape me. I still have visions of that night. I barely escaped. I believe God was with me even then.

It was after that when I began to realize my worth. I began recognizing that I was more than the words and discrimination of my neighbors, I was more than the bullies wanted me to believe, I was more than the rejection and abandonment I felt from my family. Deep within me I knew there was a plan for my life. I knew that it was time to begin that path....

THE MOMENT I REALIZED MY CALLING

As a little girl I watched a lot of movies. I would find myself watching for more than just the stories; I started observing and critiquing the details of the filming, the different camera angles and the acting styles. I would pick out some of the continuity mistakes. I developed a fascination for Hollywood. My first year of high school, I knew I wanted to focus on filmmaking and everything associated with it. I remember adding, "Hollywood, here I come!" as the caption under my senior yearbook photo. After graduating from high school I enrolled at Columbia College, the best film school in Chicago. A year later, I moved to Oklahoma and attended Oral Roberts University, where I could stay close to my faith while taking film classes. After college, I moved back to Chicago, but I wasn't sure what my next move would be.

One day my mom came into my room with an ad from our local newspaper that said, "looking for the next Miss Latina." It was an ad for a beauty pageant. I laughed. There was no way! Somehow my mom convinced me to participate. Seventy girls competed and I won 1st place runner-up. As a result, I met a talent agent who signed me on the spot. A month later I booked my first commercial. After booking a few more local commercials and a local television show, I decided it was time to "go big."

In 1996, I made the move to Hollywood. I didn't really have a plan, but I had my SAG card in tow and was ready for whatever came next. Within six months, I acquired an agent and a manager, and I booked my first feature film, called "Eight Heads in a Duffel Bag," starring Joe Pesci. Soon after that I booked several national commercials and guest-starring roles on "Friends," "Family Matters," "Suddenly Susan," "The Young and the Restless," and many more. I was on a roll! Then, one day I was approached by a record producer. He asked me if I was interested in being part of a four-girl Latin group. The next thing I knew I was in a girl band managed by Suzanne DePasse, a Motown executive, and we ended up signing a $1.3 million record deal.

Even with the accomplishments and the excitement of living my dream, something began stirring inside of me. I felt like I was losing myself…my purpose. I made the hard decision to walk away from the band to pursue my calling. That's when I was introduced to the Dream Center, a volunteer-driven organization that finds and fills the needs of individuals and families. That was it: that's what I wanted to do for the rest of my life.

In 2001, I began volunteering at the Dream Center, teaching kids in the inner city of Los Angeles how to use a film camera, edit, and host. A few months later, I went on my first mission trip to Peru with the Dream Center, which changed my life forever. Seeing so many people in dire need of life's essentials turned my life upside down. I knew then that every project I did from that point forward was going to be purposeful.

Most of the work I had done to give back was on a local level, here in L.A. and my hometown of Chicago. Our home became a refuge for homeless people, people in transition, single moms.

MEETING WENDY

When I met Wendy at church, she and her husband appeared to be a regular couple. They had two young children and Wendy was expecting again. Then one Sunday I saw Wendy by herself. She looked exhausted, stressed and scared. When I asked her if she was okay, she said "No." She went on to tell me that her husband had been taken to prison for check fraud and she was about to be homeless. She had two weeks to find a place to live. I looked down at her beautiful little girl and the newborn in her arms. I had to do something to help. I knew what homelessness feels like.

I found financial assistance at my church that was called the

Benevolent Fund. Next, I contacted Wendy and took her and the children to lunch. I told her she would live with me. We would use the fund for diapers, clothes, and other needs. Then we headed to her house to get her things. When I walked in the door, I couldn't believe it. There were cockroaches all over the floor, the furniture, the clothing. We took very little. It would be a new start.

Eventually Wendy was connected with the Dream Center when they began a family floor. Wendy and her children were the first family to reside there. It was there that they were able to live and Wendy was able to complete her GED and start a new life for her and her children.

BEFRIENDING ANGEL

People around me became aware of my passion for helping people who are in need and are homeless. And that's how I met Angel. She was a meth addict in recovery.

So Angel and I began a friendship. We talked every day. I told her I wanted to know about her life, why she had gotten to such a low point and how we might figure out together her triggers and her plans for a brighter future. My girls loved her. We brought her into our family as one of our own.

Sadly, after about two months, Angel began to change. She would come home very late. She would stay out with friends from her past and sometimes bring them home with her. I knew about drug addiction because I had seen it in my own family. I knew the signs.

Eventually, Angel went back to Orange County where she reconnected with that life. This was very hard for me. I so wanted to be successful at giving her a new start. I have heard since that she is doing better.

GLOBAL AWARENESS

I knew that there was so much more world to explore. Four years ago I was invited to a charity event in Hollywood for the

Women Like Us Foundation and met Catt Sadler, their national spokesperson. I was interested in their work with mentoring teen girls. A few months later I met the founder, Linda Rendleman. We hit it off right away—kindred spirits. I loved what her organization did, so I decided to jump on board as a volunteer. A year later, Linda invited me on one of the Women Like Us Foundation humanitarian trips to Africa. I said yes! I knew I would not only be able to support women and children in Kenya through my open heart and hands, but I could use my skills of directing and producing films to create my first documentary.

Almost three years later, *Women Like Us. Three Journeys. One Mission. To Change the World.* was born out of that trip and initiatives led by women in the United States, as well.

MY PURPOSE

My purpose now is to live every day of my life with an open heart, to be able to love completely, with eyes wide open. I am shining my own special light on the world and those in need. I'm not going to wait for someone else to do it, I'm going to be the one who does it.

Sally Colón-Petree – Producer and Director, Dream On Productions Humanitarian

▲▲▲

Yes, Sally. You won't wait to make a difference. And neither should we. And neither do any of the women in this book.

▼▼▼

Section 2 – Sex Trafficking

❝OUR BODIES ARE THE GARDEN OF OUR SOULS.❞

Deepak Chopra

▲▲▲

I set the alarm for 12:30 a.m. I really hadn't been sleeping. Just mostly trying to rest, and to anticipate and be open to the mission I was a part of that cool November night in Los Angeles. They told me to be sure to bring a jacket, as the windows will be open a lot.

The familiar ping of a text arrived on my phone: "We'll be there soon. Want a Starbucks?" I indulged in my favorite vanilla latte…kind of ironic based on the activity I was about to experience. That latte became a symbol for me that would be remembered for years to come.

A white SUV with tinted windows pulled into the drive like a white charger in the dark of night, ready to begin its work. I was invited to go along.

There were three women waiting for me: Kyla, Monique and Monica. Kyla and Monique were the leaders, the experienced ones, the women who would teach us a lot about sex trafficking in Los Angeles in the next five hours. Monica and I were the newbies. We sat in the back seat.

When I climbed in the vehicle I gratefully accepted my latte. I was told to be careful with the 32-cup stainless steel coffee urn sitting between Monica and me. It was full of hot water…ready to go for the hot chocolate we'd be handing out to the girls.

We were also handed small bags, each filled with one lip gloss with an 800 number on it, hand sanitizer, and wet wipes. In the front seat, Monique had a bag of mittens and gloves to keep hands warm against this cold night.

We turned south on the 110 and headed toward Long Beach, then on to Santa Ana/Anaheim. The Orange County area. I asked Kyla why we were leaving the inner city of Los Angeles and heading toward the suburbs. We were headed toward Disneyland, for heaven's sake. She told me I'd understand when I got there.

It was now nearing 1 a.m. Driving along a busy street in Santa Rosa we saw a few young girls dressed like they had been out for a night of "clubbing." Were they on their way home? They walked across the busy lanes of the well-lit retail area and into a residential neighborhood. Kyla stopped at the light and we watched them disappear into the darkness.

"Look ahead; see all those cars going into that neighborhood? Do you see their taillights? Do you see how they are all turning left? Those are johns."

We pulled across the street and took our place in line with them. It felt like we were in the drive-thru at McDonald's, waiting our turn. And when we made our left turn into the neighborhood, we became part of a mass of cars, all with one driver; some old, some young, some Mercedes, some rusty old trashy cars…all sharing the same common denominator of seeking sex for hire. It was a mid-month Friday night. Payday—when not so many bills were due, when child support had been paid, rent and utilities already taken care of. So, extra money meant more to spend on sex.

Monica and I were told not to speak to the girls. We were instructed to be quiet in the back seat. We were told to make them hot chocolate if they wanted it, to make no comments, to let them be them.

It's not that I didn't understand sex trafficking or that I didn't know the data. It's not that I didn't understand what the statistics were on DMST (domestic minor sex trafficking) or the realities of how women get trapped into this work, are abused by their pimps or by the johns, and treated as criminals by the police. I had studied the subject, had even spoken to hundreds of people in the Midwest and my home state of Indiana, about how it is a problem in the U.S., in our communities, and we must do something. I helped dispel the myth, or should I say the blindness, that permeates our daily, safe lives, that these things only happen in third-world countries.

They call it "the game." The game of pimps owning girls, pimps competing with one another to steal their girls, pimps patrolling the streets to make sure the girls don't talk to the competition. If the girls talk to the competition, it can be dangerous. They can be abused, cut, made to pay in a number of ways.

Sophia was the first girl I met. She was standing by herself at the edge of the street, waiting for a car to pull over and invite her in. Dressed in a red mini skirt, a black faux fur vest with a black bra underneath, and spike black and silver high heels, she walked over to us when we rolled down the window. "Hi," said Monique. "Would you like a gift?" How about some hot chocolate? Pretty cold out there tonight, isn't it?" "Oh, yes, thank you," said Sophia.

Monica made the hot chocolate and handed it through to the front seat. Sophia peered in the back where we sat, hidden from the outside by the tinted windows. She fearfully said, "Oh, you have friends?" She pulled back a bit. "Yes," replied Monique,

"They're helping us with the hot chocolate. By the way, we know about the game. You'll find a lip gloss with an 800 number on it in the little bag." Sophia said, "OK, thanks. And thanks for the hot chocolate." She moved back to her spot on the street. Back to work.

There were 13 girls on that block that night. Some young, some older, some dressed scantily, others dressed in sweats, some Caucasian, some African American, some Hispanic…a mix of nationalities, but where we were…mostly African American. Some were boys, but mostly women.

We went to three different locations that night, including two in the inner city of Los Angeles. In all we talked with 43 girls; 37 of them accepted our gift bags that contained the 800 number. Six declined. In the three years Kyla has been going out every week, 300 women have been touched and approximately a third of them have entered social service programs.

So how does this happen? How does someone become a victim? How does someone get free? What's the process? Does this process really make a difference? What happened in someone's life to get to this point? Where are the people to help? What are the police doing? How can all of this be? What resources do we have to reach understanding…to explain the Why and the What and the How?

Sex trafficking is, by definition, when a commercial sexual act is induced by force, fraud or coercion. And when the person who performs the act is under the age of 18 years, it is a serious violation of federal law. The victims can be women or men, boys or girls. In fact, the silence is great among young men as victims; it is hard to estimate the percentage of boys enslaved in sex trafficking.

A commercial sex act includes more than prostitution. It includes pornography and sexual performances done for any item of value including drugs, food, shelter, or money. Although lower than for girls, for boys it still exists somewhere around 2 to 5%.

To drill it down, it takes at least three players to make this one of the most profitable businesses in the world: a buyer, a pimp, and a victim.

It's a simple case of supply and demand. The buyer, known often as a john, pays for a service. So, if we didn't have users, we wouldn't have victims. And if we didn't have users' pimps, we would have no business. And if the pimps had no business, they wouldn't have money and would have to find some other way to bring in the dough. And, to be Miss Obvious, if there were no business, there would be no victims.

For years, the victims (the prostitutes), have been labeled as the criminals. Rarely have pimps been criminalized and even more rarely have the johns gotten more than a slap on the hand.

So, how do the traffickers find the victims? Social media is one way. It's the information age and not all information is for the greater good. Girls are also found in their own neighborhoods, near playgrounds, hanging out at the gym, at the mall, bars and clubs. There is even a book called, *How to Be a Pimp?* It's an actual guide to sex trafficking.

SEX TRAFFICKING IS A BOOMING BUSINESS

When I met Linda Smith for the first time, I didn't realize the significance of her work with Shared Hope International. Her demeanor was businesslike. She spoke in short sentences, almost staccato. And she had an air about her that suggested she was a woman with a mission. I learned about Linda Smith through a friend who was championing awareness of sex trafficking, particularly in the United States. I knew Linda was a former Congresswoman and that she was working hard to promote more stringent laws to fight sex trafficking. I knew we needed to learn more about her work.

In 2013 the Super Bowl came to Indianapolis. With all the restaurants, hotels, city services, and tourism departments excited about the upcoming game, the city was buzzing. Preparations were being made as the spotlight was shining on the community.

We were unaware that around the nation, pimps and johns were excited about the upcoming Super Bowl, too. The pimps were making their own preparations for the festivities, where in one weekend, hundreds of thousands of people were to show up in one place—and many of them would be johns. The pimps' preparations included finding locations for their girls and marketing their product in Indianapolis that weekend.

Some girls come to this work willingly. It's part of their lifestyle. Some are freshly trafficked…picked up by someone they think is their new boyfriend, driven across state lines, forced into sex and frightened for their lives.

Many think about trafficking as if it only exists outside of the United States. It makes our hearts sad, but what can we do? Many concerned individuals travel to Cambodia, India, Thailand or other third-world countries to try to help. It's overwhelming and it seems impossible. Many girls have been kidnapped and imprisoned. And we ask ourselves, *Does that one child I may be able to help even make a dent in the overall problem?*

In Nicholas Kristof's *New York Times* article "What About American Girls Sold on the Streets?" he reminds us that:

> *"…we see girls all the time who have been trafficked. But in the U.S. these girls are not locked in cages or imprisoned physically, but rather they're often runaways out on the street wearing short skirts or busting out of low-cut tops, and many Americans perceive them not as trafficking victims but as miscreants who*

have chosen their way of life. So even when they're 14 years old, we often arrest and prosecute them, even as the trafficker goes free."

And he goes on to remind us that human trafficking in America and Cambodia are more similar than we would want to admit. The girls on the streets appear to be in charge, selling sex because they want to. But in reality they are often imprisoned, as well, by a pimp who is violent and takes every penny they earn.

TEENAGE PROSTITUTION IS A HUMAN RIGHTS PROBLEM

Typically, she's a 13-year-old girl of color from a troubled home who is on bad terms with her mother. Then her mom's boyfriend hits on her, and she runs away to the bus station, where the only person on the lookout for girls like her is a pimp. He buys her dinner, gives her a place to stay and next thing she knows she's earning him $1,500 a day.

THE GIRLS AREN'T CRIMINALS. THEY ARE VICTIMS.

Sex traffickers often subject their victims to bondage by debt, an illegal practice in which the traffickers tell their victims that they owe money, and that they must pledge their personal services to repay the debt. Often these debts are for housing and food.

The psychological harms are many. They include mind/body separation/disassociated ego states, shame, grief, fear, distrust, hatred of men, self-hatred, and suicidal thoughts. Even PTSD (Post-Traumatic Stress Disorder), which includes acute anxiety, depression, insomnia, physical hyper-alertness, and self-loathing that are long-lasting and resistant to change.

In an effort to understand the problem more thoroughly, I invited former Congresswoman Linda Smith to speak at our annual women's event in Indianapolis. And through this one event, she opened my eyes and the eyes of 400 women in the room that day to the problems of sex trafficking in the United States.

▼▼▼

▲▲▲

Linda Smith is utilizing her education, her skills and her heart to stand strongly against the traffickers and the johns, and her work is making a difference. Since 2011 her organization has been evaluating the effectiveness of our states with regard to the criminalization of users and traffickers, protection of the children and effectiveness of the laws. Over the past five years, more awareness on the supply and demand of sex trafficking and new laws that are more stringent give hope that there will be more control of this billion-dollar industry and social justice for the victims.

▼▼▼

Linda Smith

CHANGING STATE LAW— HELPING THE VICTIMS

❝ I CERTAINLY DIDN'T WANT TO DRAMATICALLY CHANGE MY LIFE. ❞

I didn't want to touch the foul-smelling girl. I certainly didn't want to dramatically change my life again.

Just four years earlier, while I was on vacation, I'd been sent to Congress in an unprecedented write-in campaign launched by a few loyal friends. Now my days were crammed with policy and serving my constituents as Congresswoman Linda Smith, representing Washington State's Third Congressional District.

It was one phone call to my office that forever changed my course. A missionary had called to tell me about the commercial sex industry and forced prostitution that was occurring in India. I had to see for myself. After our conversation, I couldn't sleep; images of innocent and exploited children were invading my mind and dreams. Could it really be as bad as he said? I would soon discover it was worse than I could have imagined or believed. In the midst of my hectic schedule, five days opened up for me to squeeze in a trip to India.

On Falkland Road in Mumbai, I was stunned by the reality of the sex trade industry. Women and children lined streets where raw sewage flowed in uncovered ditches. I found young girls, mere children, locked in rooms deep within brothels, or several stories up behind barred windows, waiting for men who "like them young."

"THE CONDITIONS OF HER LIFE WERE DEPLORABLE... I KNEW I HAD TO DO SOMETHING."

One girl in particular impacted me. She was a wisp of a thing, filthy, alone. The conditions of her life were deplorable. The scent of a thousand men was upon her. She looked to be about the age of my granddaughter. "I am doomed forever," her eyes said. "Beyond help. Beyond hope." Then I heard a still, small voice telling me to touch her. I denied it but the voice returned. Finally I reached for her. My mind had changed already, shocked and scarred by the images I'd seen.

But, in the instant I touched this child, she fell into my arms and my heart was branded. Feeling the frail humanity of her heartbeat against mine, I knew I had to do something.

I discovered many of these little girls had been brought to India all the way from Nepal. As impossible as it seemed, most were sold by their own parents, duped into believing they'd have good work and a better life. Others had been kidnapped or stolen. In every case, the cause was the same: Someone had to supply product for the hungry sex markets in Mumbai.

My heart broke for those little Nepalese girls. They wanted to go home to their own culture, to familiar food, to a familiar climate. So we began opening homes in Nepal, as well.

India and Nepal were only a first taste, only an introduction into the human trafficking and sex trade industry. I would soon find this horror stretches around the world. I came into a new, perhaps even more awful, shock: this nightmare was happening in my own back yard. This wasn't an India problem. It wasn't an international problem. It was a United States problem.

SHARED HOPE INTERNATIONAL

Within weeks after my trip to India I created Shared Hope International, a non-profit corporation. With my husband, Vern, and as many friends as I could convince to join us, we combined assets and resources to create homes for girls, like the one I held in my arms that night.

Shared Hope International first actively addressed sex trafficking of American children through researching the markets creating demand for commercial sex. The Demand Project investigated buyers, facilitators, and traffickers in four countries: Jamaica, Japan, the Netherlands, and the United States. The startling findings highlighted the fact that sex trafficking is demand-driven, and the product for sale is most often local, domestic children. Dedicated to ending the human rights violation of sex trafficking internationally and domestically, Shared Hope International received a grant from the U.S. Department of Justice to perform field research on domestic minor sex trafficking and the commercial sexual exploitation of American children in the United States.

The summary of the research, *The National Report on Domestic Minor Sex Trafficking: The Prostitution of America's Children*, was read into the Congressional record in 2009 in a Congressional hearing. As I presented the key findings to my former colleagues, I summarized with these words "I looked into the trafficking market in America and saw us." Yes, we found some women and children brought across our border for the sex market, but the largest group of victims came from the middle schools of America. To summarize the findings:

Kids from all economic and ethnic backgrounds were in the commercial sex markets.

———

The buyers were American men from all ethnic and economic backgrounds.

———

The younger the youth the more men will pay.

———

The kids were being criminalized and arrested for prostitution.

———

The men who shop for kids were being charged with a misdemeanor, if charged at all.

———

Then, I met "Lacy." Just a few months before being sold, 12-year-old Lacy was excelling in school and loved going to her church youth group. Her dad was in Iraq. Her mom often worked overtime, so she watched her brother and 10-year-old sister. She was just a good kid.

A man in his early 20s hung around her school and her neighborhood until he was no longer a stranger. He listened to her, said her eyes twinkled, and told her she was much more mature than her age. By age 13 she secretly considered him her boyfriend. She was sold to five men the first night he decided to turn her into cash. Then he showed her the pictures he'd taken. He threatened her with exposure. He labeled her a criminal and warned that criminals get arrested. If she spoke to the police, he'd grab her 10-year-old sister.

CHANGING STATE LAW - HELPING THE VICTIMS

It became very clear to me that all my state and federal policy experience was needed if I were to help girls like Lacy. While federal law was strong and beginning to be enforced by the FBI and U.S. attorneys across America, it was state law that allowed Lacy to be charged as a prostitute and denied her the justice and services a victim of violent crime should receive.

Without significant law changes in all 50 states, we wouldn't be able to call on our law enforcement and prosecutors to protect Lacy and bring her justice. Without law changes, the state child welfare agencies would consider her a criminal. They wouldn't provide her appropriate housing, counseling, or advocacy she needed as a victim of numerous violent crimes. Armed with our research, legal experts from many states, and several third-year law students, Shared Hope's legal team wrote legal briefs and recommendations on each state to help guide the creation of domestic minor sex trafficking laws.

The *Protected Innocence Challenge* was designed to build a legal framework established on individual states' legal systems to protect children from traffickers and to bring justice and restoration to youth victimized by this horrible crime. All states received a letter grade on the strength of their law. The first report cards gave failing grades to most of the states; only a few were above a C. Now, five years later, most states have C grades or above. State activists and lawmakers have used this legal work across the nation to strengthen their laws. As a result, it's now a felony nationwide to buy sex from a minor. I didn't set out to be a member of Congress. I didn't plan to establish Shared Hope International. I didn't even want to go to India at first. Something within prompted me to go. Once there, the situation overwhelmed me. It was so much bigger than me. I felt unprepared to take on such incredible work. How could I cope with a problem of such magnitude? Then a still, small voice reminded me of a valuable lesson: God doesn't rely on my will. He just asks that I show up—and obey that urge to step forward.

"Just show up and let a God bigger than me do the rest."

When I asked a friend to help me build the first village, she asked, "What are you going to do with the girls?" This question rang in my memory, but I know God compelled me to "just show up." That's what I was determined to do. Within weeks of the first night in Mumbai, 37 women and children were in our safe houses in India and Nepal. Most of these women are now living full lives.

Vern and I were just honored to be involved in the wedding of one of these first girls, only seven years old when pulled out of that dark place. She has graduated from college with a degree in social work and now works at the Village of Hope where she grew up. Lacy is a mom and wife living a life of choices… not slavery. Not because I had the perfect plan, education, or talents. I just was willing to show up and let a God bigger than me do the rest.

Linda Smith-Founder Shared Hope International

▲▲▲

Leadership can make an impact, whether through legislation or development of big organizations like Shared Hope International or a personal passion working on one's own like Kyla Smith….

When I went on that ride in the dark of night in Los Angeles and met those women and girls on the street, it was Kyla Smith at the wheel. It was Kyla Smith who had the grit and the impetus to spend several nights a week offering friendship and resources to the trafficked women. I learned a lot about "the game" from her that night. I wanted to learn more about this special person who loved so greatly. I asked her to tell it to me and all of us.

▼▼▼

Kyla Smith

LOVE AND COURAGE FOR A BETTER WORLD

> **"**GIRL," HE SAID, "**YOU LIKE TO LOVE**, DON'T YOU?"
> "WELL, YES...YES I DO!" I SAID.**"**

I was aware of bullying from a young age. I saw the pain in the face of my good friend when it happened to her. And it happened to her by a group of girls I thought were also my friends. Somehow I felt responsible. I had remorse and guilt for being friends with bullies. I felt my own pain and wanted to make it right. I do believe that was the first moment when I understood how important it was for me to make people feel loved and included.

The threads of how I felt because of that instance in childhood have carried through my life.

The birth of my oldest sister was a touch-point for my family. You see, my parents had no idea prior to birth that their beautiful baby girl had spina bifida. After two surgeries they were sent home with their baby and told she would never walk, have possible brain damage/developmental delays, and multiple other health issues related to the defect. They were sent for genetic counseling and told as they sat holding their precious baby how they could be tested and end any future pregnancy if the defect was detected. They were horrified to think that the child they held and loved could have been destroyed because she wasn't "perfect" by the world's definition. But they remained steady, and their faith strong – had four more children, and my sister walked across the stage to receive her college degree.

Mom and Dad, and then all of us, got very involved in the pro-life movement in Mississippi, understanding that life doesn't have to be extinguished if an unborn baby won't be perfect. All life has its gifts…you just have to see them. And we were the lucky ones to have learned that through my sister.

Even though we didn't have a lot, we had enough. Our home was always open to pregnant women and babies. I saw the sacrifices we made again and again to help other families. And my father eventually became the president of the Mississippi Right to Life organization.

I've always felt called to be with people who are hurting. It's my nature, I guess. Or maybe my gift. I want the world to be safe and feel good. I knew in the center of my being that this would be my path.

On my own at 18, I moved to Nashville, Tennessee, where I took a job as a full-time nanny and got very involved in starting a ministry for young adults at the local church. I became the person others came to with their problems. I would help them think through things, set a plan for action, and help find resources—or I'd simply be a listener.

MEETING SUSAN

Eventually the woman who established the Hope Clinic for Women approached me. She was seeking someone to be the house mom for a home for pregnant girls. I lived with the girls, helped them through their pregnancies, oversaw a new satellite office where I managed the crisis line and generally ran the facility.

On one beautiful day in May, my crisis line phone rang. I answered, and for a few moments, I heard nothing but breathing on the other end. The caller's name was Susan. She was encouraged by her parents to abort the baby inside of her. She was young. She had a life ahead of her. A baby was coming too soon in her world. Susan's boyfriend didn't want anything to do with her. She started talking to me. I mostly listened. Then she hung up. An hour later she called back. We talked some more. She was scheduled for an abortion in a couple of days. She just needed to talk. After the third call I asked her to come by and said I'd listen more, that she could keep talking. When she arrived (I'll never forget the beautiful day), we sat outside at a picnic table under a shady oak tree…and I continued to listen.

In the end, Susan kept her baby. She moved into the home with us and went through her pregnancy there. Because of our conversations that day, she realized there could still be a life for her baby, but without her. She wasn't ready to be a mom. There would be someone who would love the baby the way she should be loved.

It was a personal gift for me, and a wonderful opportunity, to help her with the open adoption process…finding the right family, selecting who would love and raise her baby.

When the day of birth came, I was there with her. In fact, the little baby girl came so quickly (the doctor wasn't even there yet) that I caught her by her little foot before she fell off the birthing table. In some ways, I felt we had this child together.

I was with Susan as she went through the grieving process. And I was with her at the ceremony in a beautiful chapel where she handed over the child to the new parents. What I saw that day was one of the most selfless acts of love and courage I had ever seen. Susan was my first real hero.

I have no contact with Susan today, but I just know she is living her life well and making thoughtful decisions like she did that year.

After two years at the maternity home, due to lack of funds

and other requirements for such a facility, my position changed. This was very hard for me. Running the home had been my dream job. Yet, when one door closes…

IT WAS ONE OF THE HARDEST THINGS I'VE EVER DONE

My phone rang out of the blue. It was a woman named Pam who had heard about my work. She wanted to talk. And that's how I became a mastectomy fitter at a store called Pretty in Pink Boutique. I made the transition from women who were making life or death decisions for their babies to women with breast cancer who were fighting for their own lives.

I worked with women who had just been diagnosed, women who may not have even told their families yet, women who didn't know how long they had to live. Sometimes the doctor tells them they will need the mastectomy and sends them for a fitting immediately. This job was one of the hardest things I've ever done in my life. This type of work wears on you. I learned to have the utmost respect for the women working with me and the women who held onto their hope and their faith with courage as they went through this ordeal.

PHIL WAS ON SKID ROW

He was like a seven-year-old girl in Kobe Bryant's body. His name was Phil and he was draped in all types of layers—including some little girls' clothing or whatever he could find on the street on Skid Row. I'd decided to go on a mission trip with my church to help the homeless in Los Angeles. As I poured him coffee, asking if he wanted sugar and cream, I looked up to see his eyes locked on mine. "Girl," he said, "You like to love, don't you?" "Well, yes…yes I do!" I said.

Working with the homeless that short time was very life-giving for me. I felt a freedom in living from day to day and being with those who had nothing. It was meaningful to show up every day and offer a little bit of light and hope. And when

I went back home to Nashville, I felt blessed to have a home and a bed. But after a few days, each time I looked at my bed, I remembered those on the streets. I felt called to go back and do what little I could for them.

Skid Row was the darkest place I had ever been. There was a longing in me to do more—whatever it would take to make the world a better place.

So, I decided to give my life away. Whatever I had, I let it go. My clothing, my car…I packed my life in two suitcases. Leaving Nashville was a big sacrifice for me, but I knew it was the right thing to do.

THEY WERE DRESSED IN HIGH HEELS AND NO PANTIES

I call Los Angeles my third-world city. People come there for the glitz and glam. They don't know what's in the underbelly. But I do. And that's how I learned about sex trafficking. I learned about it at the Dream Center, a refuge for the homeless, in the heart of the city.

When I came to the Dream Center they had a special place for victims of human trafficking. I had never realized, like so many, that sex trafficking happens right here in the United States. I always thought it took place only in third-world countries. I had, of course, heard about prostitution, but I didn't know whether sex trafficking was different or the same. I had always heard that prostitution is a choice. I learned that's not so. "Prostitutes" often are the product of sex trafficking. It's not a decision.

I wanted to see for myself. I wanted to learn more about "the life" on the "game," as they called it. I wanted to help with rescue and recovery. I wanted to understand.

I sought out a location where I had been told the girls were being trafficked and drove there on a Sunday morning at 2 a.m. I saw about eight girls on the streets. They were wearing next to nothing. No panties, high heels, little skirts…that's it. The girls were looking for johns (the customers). As I looked across the street from the girls, I saw several men I assumed were pimps (traffickers)...watching over their stables (the girls).

I heard a girl shout out, "Hot!" which is a warning that the police were spotted. There was a scurry of running across the street where the pimps were. The pimps wouldn't help them. Then they were running back to the other corner where the police had arrived to arrest them. Then back to the pimps looking for protection. It was a desperate attempt to flee, but there was nowhere to go. They were being herded like cattle between their traffickers and law enforcement who treat them as criminals due to a lack of understanding about how "the game" works.

IT WAS THAT EVENING THAT MOTIVATED ME TO MAKE A PLAN

I talked to law enforcement, other organizations, joined task forces and began by locating the areas in Los Angeles where girls were being sold on the streets. The place to start was to try to get to know the girls and let them know we were there to help them when they were ready—and then to give the girls a place to go. And, of course, to make them feel safe when they were there. But to get that done, the girls needed to be educated, and in turn, educate one another.

I started with driving to the areas where the girls worked. I built a relationship with them by offering little gift bags with lip gloss and an 800 number. I would tell them we were there if they ever "needed anything" in an attempt to get them to call the number and offer them a way "out of the life." Eventually the girls recognized my SUV and would walk up to me to say hello. I established trust. I cared about them, and they knew it. Yet we were always mindful of the pimps—lurking, watching, patrolling the streets to make sure the girls were working. They are his paycheck. I could never stop for very long.

Through the Dream Center we worked to set up an

emergency shelter. At the time, it was the only one in the city. There they have a safe place to rest, make decisions for themselves, and determine or at least think about what they want to do and how they can move forward to a better life. And in order to get them there, we created a rescue team that is available 24/7. We pick them up wherever they are.

We partnered with law enforcement and other recovery programs in the city and across the U.S. that focus on the specific needs of stabilizing each individual girl. Once through the programs, typically in about six months, they go to a transitional program for entry back into the world.

Through our program at the Dream Center we have rescued over 300 girls in just three years.

And that's my story for now. We're creating awareness in the city of Los Angeles. We're amassing volunteers who have the heart to help eradicate the fastest growing criminal business in the world.

I'm helping sex-trafficked victims become sex-trafficked survivors. I'm using my gifts of love and courage for a better world.

Kyla Smith-Activist and Humanitarian

▲▲▲

K.D. was a victim of familial trafficking. The awareness and reporting of it is just emerging. It's sometimes reported as child sexual abuse, yet as more education is available for prosecutors, social workers and people on the front lines, the trafficking of a minor by family members is getting attention and legislation to help with change.

K.D. found her way back to health with professional assistance and, although as she admits, forever damaged, she's loving greatly and standing strongly against sexual abuse and trafficking. And she doesn't dwell on what happened behind her, but rather what is her present and her future. K.D. speaks to groups about her story, including her LGBT lifestyle and her message of the world coming together with love and compassion for all.

▼▼▼

K.D. Roche
WHY DIDN'T YOU TELL SOMEONE?

❝ I CANNOT SHARE MY PAST WITH MOST PEOPLE. ❞

My name is K.D. Roche. I am a mother, professional career woman, college student, published author, and a survivor of human trafficking. My trafficking took place during childhood from the ages of eight to sixteen years old. The gruesome details are unimportant. What is important is that my innocence was stolen from me before I was old enough to multiply and divide. My trafficking involved family members, and unfortunately, is much more common than America would like to admit. As is true for many survivors of sex-trafficking, I experienced sexual abuse prior to my body being sold for sex. This positioned me to be vulnerable for further exploitation, which eventually led to being forced into pornography and then being sold for sex throughout my childhood and adolescence.

I used to tell the details of my experience, but have since stopped doing so for two reasons: 1.) It is not only re-traumatizing to tell my story, but it can be traumatic also to the reader, and 2.) there is a tendency for the media and public to sensationalize the topic of human trafficking and the stories of those who have endured it. According to the *Oxford Dictionary*, "Sensationalism" is defined as (especially in journalism) "the use of exciting or shocking stories or language at the expense of accuracy, in order to provoke public interest or excitement." Although the reality of my story (and others' stories) are often considered shocking to the general public, the graphic details that nab the attention of readers is not what I am after. I am after social change, public education, child advocacy, human rights, and the abolition of modern-day slavery.

I urge you, instead of gobbling up heart-wrenching stories as if they were juicy tabloids, to respect the fact that trauma survivors do not want to be re-traumatized by the re-telling of their stories. Families do not want to see the graphic details written about in books, posted on the internet, or regurgitated on the news. Instead, let's focus on what we can do to educate ourselves about the problem and to help those who have experienced it.

In response to many questions one might have in regards to my childhood trafficking, an excerpt from the short story that I authored myself can be found in chapter 4 of *Made in the USA*, by Alisa Jordheim.

> *"I cannot share my past with most people. They just wouldn't understand. And even on the rare occasion I open up in the slightest, the response I receive is a load of questions. Simple questions. Common questions. Painful questions. "Why didn't you tell someone?" "Why didn't you call the police?" "Why did you go back?" "Why didn't you turn them in?" Valid questions, I guess, to a person who doesn't understand, but wounding questions to a victim of violence. These questions insinuate that I could have ended the abuse at any point in time, that I chose it for myself, that I never tried to escape—or worse, that it was either consensual or it was a lie (otherwise I would have reported it). These are the questions that simplify*

what is not simple at all. These are the questions of an individual who has never been beaten, broken, and brutalized; silenced, drugged, or locked up; burned, cut, or on the hollow end of a gun barrel. These are the questions of one who has never seen an officer, politician, or respected husband and father at the back room of a brothel."

Today, I spend my time training, educating, and addressing the problem of human trafficking in the United States. I have trained law enforcement, social workers, government workers, juvenile justice judges, therapists, and the public on ways to recognize trafficking situations, promote policy work that protects victims of human trafficking, and treat and care for survivors of sexual exploitation in a way that is trauma-informed and effective. You may access my training videos and materials on my website: www.freetobemedmst.com, subscribe to my YouTube channel: K.D. Roche, or like my Facebook page: K.D. Roche to keep informed on the issue of human trafficking and how you can help.

Some of us don't think we have much to give, or realize we can make a difference. Some of us don't know how to even begin. But if you listen to your heart, you'll find the answers waiting for you. That's what happened to Jessica. A young woman with a big gift, she saw a need, listened to her internal voice and stepped out in faith to make a difference in her community. It's not that we have to change the entire world, but we CAN make a difference right where we live. One person at a time. Here's her story.

Jessica Evans

PURCHASED

> ❝ I STARTED TO UNDERSTAND THAT GREAT LEADERS AREN'T JUST THE ONES ON STAGE WITH DYNAMIC PERSONALITIES. TRULY GREAT LEADERS ARE HUMBLE SERVANTS WHO **PERSEVERE** WHEN IT GETS TOUGH. ❞

I believe some people are born with a spark inside of them: somehow they've always known they were going to change the world. They are born leaders, always looking for a mountain to climb, a problem to solve, or a crowd to lead. They are dynamic, magnetic and ready to fight whatever battle comes their way with tenacity and boldness. They, and everyone around them, know with certainty that they will make waves in the world and are eager to rise to the challenge.

I AM NOT ONE OF THOSE PEOPLE

Had you known me in my growing-up years, you would have described me as sweet, quiet, a good listener, and a committed friend. I was an honor roll student, a music lover and somewhat of a homebody. I had a close group of friends and an amazing family, went to church every Sunday and lived a pretty sheltered childhood.

One thing that was special about me was my soft heart. I cried during a movie anytime someone was sad. I focused all my projects in school on homelessness, Harriett Tubman and the underground railroad. I read every book I could get my hands on about people who suffered. I cried for them and wished I could help them.

I fell into the education field partly because of my desire to love and care for children, and partly because I come from a family of teachers. Throughout my nine years in the classroom, I was always drawn to those kiddos who needed extra love, attention and support. I thought I had found my calling in life: to make a difference in the lives of kindergarten students, through teaching. What I didn't know, was God had another plan for me.

I HAD BEEN TOLD THESE THINGS ALL MY LIFE

Early in 2007, I began learning about human trafficking, mostly through the books I was addicted to reading. My heart was broken for these girls I read about—girls who had never been told how beautiful they are, how valuable and talented they are and how their future was full of potential if given the opportunity. I had been told these things all my life. I never questioned that I was loved or that I had someone to take care of me. I longed to be the one to hug these girls and tell them they were special and dear to someone's heart.

I got my opportunity that fall when I took a trip to Nepal and India through my church. For the first time, I met face-to-face with girls who had experienced more trauma and abuse than my 26-year-old self could imagine. I got to hug them, laugh with them, buy soap and jewelry that they lovingly handmade. What a joy, and what a humbling experience. To be honest, that trip broke me.

I remember sitting on the floor of my living room when I got home. This was not the first time I had been overseas and experienced life in a third-world country, but for some reason, this was different. I was heartbroken. As I remembered each face, and recounted each story, I felt an urgency. I needed to do something. But what? I was a kindergarten teacher in Indiana. Surely I was not being called to go overseas, but what impact could I possibly make from here? I'm no one of influence or importance; I'm just an average young schoolteacher with a soft heart. At least, that's what I thought.

One lesson I've learned is that when you pray with a sincere heart for God to use you, he will do it. That day on my living room floor changed the course of my life and I didn't even know it at that moment. For the next three or four months, I humbly and naively prayed that I could be used somehow to show these girls they are loved and valuable. I was committed to listening and paying attention to how that prayer might be answered, however big or small. I got my answer in the car on the way to visit my brother at college. I was praying and daydreaming as I cruised along on my two-hour trip, and all of a sudden had a picture in my mind of a concert. Somehow I knew in my heart it was an awareness concert about human trafficking. I also saw the names of five of my friends I was supposed to talk to about putting on this concert. I immediately thought, *What a great idea! I should tell someone they should do this!* I tried to ignore the feeling in my gut that it was a call for me, not for someone else.

I KNEW WITH CERTAINTY I WAS TO BE A LEADER

By the time I returned home from that visit, I knew with certainty that this was a call given to me personally, and it scared me. I was not someone who was often called a leader. Who would take me seriously? What did I even have to offer? But I couldn't ignore the nagging feeling in my heart that this was something I needed to do. I sheepishly emailed those 5 friends and met them for breakfast a few days later. When I described to them my idea for a concert, they were all on board and within a few weeks, a concert was in the works!

We named the concert "Purchased," and did our best to educate the 200 people who joined us about the issue of human trafficking. We called it a success, and I thought I had checked the box on the thing God had asked me to do. Only little did I know this was just the beginning.

Over the next nine years, "Purchased" began to grow. Not only did our awareness efforts grow, but I also grew. As I kept saying "yes" to each next thing, my confidence began to develop. I started to understand that great leaders aren't just the ones on stage with dynamic personalities. Truly great leaders are humble servants who persevere when it gets tough. The best leaders empower the people around them to make a difference and be their best. Leaders people want to follow are genuine, passionate and reliable. When I began to realize that I had leadership qualities inside me that just needed to be uncovered and cultivated, my response to the call to this work went from "Don't you want someone else?" to "What do we get to do next?"

While this work has been a joy and an exciting ride, jumping into the non-profit field with little experience has had its challenges. I'm on a constant learning curve that I've come to love. As we continue to grow, there's always something new to learn and a challenge to overcome. The best part of this journey has been that from day one I've been able to walk it with a team. The power of joining with others cannot be overstated. What I lack, others can provide. When I'm discouraged, others can carry the load. We are in this together, and it's a blessing. I've walked the road of quitting my teaching job as an act of faith and committing to this work full-time. For two years, my community surrounded me, believed in me, helped me pay my bills and bridged the gap until I could be fully employed by our organization. I could not have done it alone.

The best nuggets of advice I could give are these: First, pay attention to what breaks your heart. Don't let fear get in your way of taking action. No matter who you are or where you are, you can make some kind of difference, some kind of impact, however big or small. Second, don't do it alone. Find a team, your squad, tribe, crew—whoever they are—and dive in together and be committed to supporting each other. You'll do far more with others than you can ever do alone.

Believe me, someone who was the most unlikely leader: you can be used in mighty ways if you allow it.

Jessica Evans-Founder of Purchased

▲▲▲

Some women write books; some start charities; some volunteer; some use their profession to make a difference. So many women are standing up to eradicate sex trafficking.
I met Shaunestte, a young attorney working in the public sector in this fight. She finds the girls, prosecutes the pimps and strives every day to create awareness and educate the public about the issue right in the middle of the U.S.A.—in Indiana.

▼▼▼

Shaunestte Terrell

WHAT THESE GIRLS WANT IS LOVE

❝ I HAVEN'T MET ONE PROSTITUTE THAT DIDN'T START OUT AS A VICTIM OF SEXUAL ABUSE. ❞

I knew I wanted to be a lawyer since I was six years old. I grew up in a blue-collar family. My father died of cancer when I was 11 and my mom struggled with mental illness. At 30 years old, my mother had no education and four kids to care for. I knew there was more in life. And I set out to make it happen for myself.

It was an incident when I was in the 6th grade that led me to becoming an attorney. After school, I went to my friend's house to play. Her parents were divorced and her dad was a deadbeat. When I walked in I saw her mother hovering over piles of papers on the dining room table, struggling to understand what they meant, and frustrated by her situation. The electric company had shut off the power to their home. There were overdue medical bills. No child support had been received in months. Yet her mother couldn't afford an attorney. She was confused and sad as she tried to understand how she could get some help from the legal system. I thought to myself how unfair this was. That day there was a fire stoked inside of me that has never gone away. It was at that moment that I knew I wanted to be an attorney, 100 percent dedicated to public service.

When I completed my undergraduate degree and prior to law school, I took a break by working for AmeriCorps with HIV/AIDS work. Eventually my positions led me to the prosecutor's office, and after several areas of focus, I was glad to take on my current role that allows me to help rescue victims, and prosecute perpetrators, of sex trafficking.

My goals as a sex trafficking prosecutor are to facilitate getting help for the girls, and to arrest the trafficker and put him away. Currently it is difficult to establish cases and arrest the johns (the clients). If we can cut the demand, we can cut the crime. But we need more female officers to get this done. We need more manpower. It is in our minds and we are eager to expand on this.

PROSTITUTES START OUT AS VICTIMS

Sometimes people are under the impression that prostitution is different from sex trafficking of a minor. But I have not met one prostitute who didn't start out as a victim of sexual abuse in some way. And, if they are older, they have just been in the system longer. They are probably more damaged, more addicted. If we confront them and they will talk to us, and give us information, we either don't charge them or will dismiss their cases. We have to try.

It's very rare that we have a victim immediately say "yes" to prosecution of the trafficker. They come from dire circumstances. They are missing something at home or they wouldn't be so easy to exploit; no money, no dad, mom is working three jobs and is an addict, lack of supervision at home. The trafficker knows that what these girls want more than anything else in the world is love, stability, loyalty…and he coerces them into believing that he will give it to them, that he will fill the voids in their life. There was a saying I heard once that went something like, "Once you own the mind, you own the body." This is what victimizers do. They know their victims' vulnerabilities, they get into their victims' minds, and they eventually control their bodies. They sell them love, sell them dreams, then they are like putty in their hands. They give them a sense of family. It doesn't start out where it ends up.

When we rescue a victim, she is typically not cooperative at first. In the beginning, we create as much distance between the victim and the trafficker as we can. We allow them to take their time, to take time away from the situation so they can start processing what has happened to them. As time passes, they begin to realize that what they have been subjected to is wrong…what was done to them was wrong. Yet some have been through so many struggles, even outside of trafficking, they are very hardened and don't know or can't comprehend that they have been victimized. Their sense of self-worth doesn't exist. This is why it is crucial to have the cooperation between local police, the U.S. Attorney, the FBI and service organizations, which solely work with sex trafficking. It is important for us to partner with facilities for at-risk youth, like a group home, where everyone understands these girls are victims, not criminals. We do not arrest them, they are not charged. Our goal is to try to help them.

PEOPLE NEED TO BE MORE AWARE

In my opinion the biggest problem we face in this country is lack of awareness. People don't believe that sex trafficking takes place here: in our neighborhoods, in our communities, in our cities, in our schools, in our families, in our lives. Kids are recruited through social media, they are recruited walking down the street, at bus stops, in malls, even at the playground. I have to craft my plea negotiations to look different depending on what court my case lands in. Each court has a different amount of understanding of the situation and I craft my plea agreements accordingly.

The legislation in Indiana is getting better. In fact, it's pretty good. If a person gets charged with promotion of human trafficking of a minor in Indiana, this means under the age of 18, whether there is consent or not, most can get anywhere from three to 16 years. But the same crime in the federal system is 30 years to life. That's why, of course, we try to get the feds involved as much as we can. I love when cases are filed federally.

Cases are also difficult to investigate and try in front of a jury due to lack of awareness. Many times the jurors are not sympathetic to the victim because the victim doesn't fit into a nice little box. Many victims don't have a clean background. Or they are not a part of the community, but rather are transient. Sometimes they have been involved in sexual abuse their whole lives; they have tattoos, facial piercings, they look like "losers." And we only get approximately 20 minutes to educate the jurors during the selection process before we start the case. Asking jurors what they know about sex trafficking in 20 minutes doesn't allow much understanding of this topic. In the questioning, the place I have to start is asking, "What do you think of when you hear the term 'human trafficking'?"

The way the law reads in Indiana, sex trafficking is human trafficking. It's a bit of a misnomer. When you say this to a jury, many think of a girl from overseas locked in a truck against her will. And that is the way it needs to be presented in the courts. But most of my cases are sex trafficked teenage girls from our own back yard who are vulnerable in many different ways and from many different situations.

The media is so important for spreading awareness. Organizations creating awareness at a grass-roots level is important. Educating our children in our schools is important. It's all a part of protecting our kids and prosecuting the bad guys. Yet we struggle with the lack of understanding and lack of awareness in the general population. And the problem is increasing. My case load keeps growing. I have three more traffickers to charge within the next week.

FINDING THE VICTIMS

We find the girls in several ways, but mostly through Backstage.com, a website that the pimps use to market the girls. For the trafficked, under-age girls, they use words like: young, new, fresh. If they state, "no black guys," that can be a signal they have a pimp. We look for these buzzwords, look for girls who look young, set up equipment in hotels, and do as they do with adults. Then an overnight sting is set up. One of our team sets an appointment and will follow the trail. Sometimes the pimps are found parked nearby. Sometimes he signs her into a hotel and is on the registry. Once we get the agreement, that is the act. The crime of prostitution is in the agreement, not the actual act. An arrest can take place right away or sometimes it takes months.

Other resources for finding victims include 800 numbers, but honestly, since I've been in my position, we have not had one call on our 800 cell line. We do get referrals from Child Protective Services and we get a lot of mothers who know their daughter is at a hotel and the name of a boyfriend who took her there. We also get referrals when a social worker suspects a child is being trafficked.

I met a girl last December who was 20, on a night we picked up streetwalkers. They all were so messed up. They were all addicted to drugs. One girl said she had a pimp, but her mother took the pimp away from her, saying, "I'm a better hooker than you." I hope we can stop a 13- or 14-year-old from becoming that girl I met.

Shaunestte Terrell - Deputy Prosecuting Attorney, Human Trafficking Missing Persons Division

WHAT CAN YOU DO?

1. Become more informed.

---

2. Volunteer for an organization that fights sex trafficking in your community.

---

3. Know the signs of a trafficked child.

---

4. Be proactive in reporting suspicious activity.

---

5. Don't look the other way.

---

6. Be an advocate for victims.

Section 3 – Homelessness

> ❝...THE GREATEST SUFFERING IS BEING LONELY, FEELING UNLOVED, HAVING NO ONE...THAT IS THE WORST DISEASE THAT ANY HUMAN BEING CAN EVER EXPERIENCE. ❞
>
> Mother Teresa

▲▲▲

Homelessness comes in many forms. I've seen it on the streets of India, on the streets of Los Angeles, under the railroad trestles in Indiana, in the upscale city of Honolulu, and at a zillion overpasses and exits off the freeway where desperate moms, dads and children hold up cardboard signs asking for help. I've seen it while volunteering at homeless shelters, bringing meals to the needy, building homes in the Dominican Republic and holding hands with homeless girls and orphans in Africa.

It's a hard thing. Wanting to help but not knowing how, offering a few dollars that makes no difference, really, at all. No real difference.

WE ARE ONE

My children and I love Thanksgiving. It's our favorite holiday because it's about appreciating our lives, and being thankful for the ones we love and our simple blessings. And so, over the years, we've made Thanksgiving Day sort of an "outreach" from our family to the world.

Years ago, when my children were quite small, we adopted a family in need in our little Midwest town. With kids in tow, wearing their hats, mittens and boots to ward off the snowy night, we went to the local IGA grocery store and loaded up our basket with canned goods, a turkey, fresh bread, cool milk and crunchy vegetables…all for a family we didn't know, but we had been told they needed help. Off we went to find the address. Their rented home had been given to them for a few dollars a month until they could get on their feet.

I have to admit I was a little nervous as our family, each member carrying a grocery bag, knocked on the door. I wanted to convey my respect, preserve the dignity of this family, and the understanding that one of the greatest gifts we can give to one another while we are here on earth is love, compassion and a sense of "we are in this world as one, all here to be a part of one another's journey."

When the door opened, a man, woman and two small children stood in front of us. They were quiet. They were thankful. They invited us in. Two families, two sets of parents, all a part of humanity, the same struggles of doing the best we can for our children, never giving up, making the most of what we have. Whether you own a home, have an education, go to work every day or lose your ability to do so, the struggle and yes, the joy, for all of us is to create the best life we can.

We spoke with the family only briefly. It was awkward for them and it was awkward for us. Then we left. I had a sense of sadness and a feeling of inadequacy as I walked down the front walk to our car. "Well," I said to my children, "I am happy we could do that for them. They are a wonderful family. Some times are just hard." But my heart was aching. What else could I do? Had we done anything that really mattered? The food would disappear yet the problems remained.

I wonder where they are today?

THEY ARE YOU AND ME

Who are the homeless? How did they become homeless? Why don't they just get a job? Are they drug addicts? Are they uneducated or mentally ill?

And what does the word "homeless" mean in terms of the definition and categorization of people who live on the street, in shelters, in tented cities, on couches in homes of those who will take them in?

I felt it was time to really gain a true understanding that could clarify for me how this happens, with an end goal of how I and others could make a difference. I truly believe that to help with the problem, it's imperative we understand it.

Many people believe those who are homeless are not a normal part of the population, that they can't get the benefits of social welfare to help get them back on their feet. It is difficult to have an identity, an address, or a way to stay in touch or to be contacted, if you're homeless. And others assert that the homeless in the United States are a developing social group rising out of unaffordable housing due to the continuing and widening economic and wage gaps between the classes.

The homeless situation in the United States is a difficult one to define. Analytical studies in cities across the country have come up with their own statistics, their own programs for solving and helping the needs of the homeless and, yes, many opinions surface on the who, how and what of homelessness.

So I started doing my own research. And I got, if not answers, some direction and understanding of the problem, the economic concerns, the attitudes and issues from the voice of the homeless and more.

Along the way I met some outstanding women who are raising their voices and finding solutions. They are doing it with love, compassion and strength.

HOUSELESS IN HAWAII

My first real look at homelessness here at home was, of all places, Honolulu, where the average home price is $700,000 and the average rent is $2,700 a month.

I had traveled there on personal business and to visit a friend who is an attorney in the city. I began asking questions about the sustainability of the Hawaiian culture in a city so modern, and we eventually spoke about the homeless problem in Honolulu. In this world of beautiful beaches, high rises, dramatic views and mansions perched on hilltops, homelessness seemed like an impossibility. But it is very real.

My friend encouraged me to take a closer look. And that is how I met Kathryn Xian, the founder and head of Pacific Alliance to Stop Slavery.

It was at a coffee shop in the heart of a wealthy retail center in Honolulu when she walked up to me. I liked her immediately. She had an air about her that was all business. She was a woman with a purpose. As we began to get to know one another, Kathryn was quick to let me know about her work and her mission for the homeless. She told me about how government leaders didn't want to deal with the homeless situation because it would hurt the tourist trade. They tried to keep it quiet. She told me that within two blocks of where we were sipping our coffee there are homeless families living in tents. She told me one of the reasons for this was the high cost of living and the low wages. These people are the working poor—the working homeless. She suggested I slip around the corner and see the community of a city of tents.

Tents are a means of survival, a shelter for sleep and a way of creating a part of a community with others in the same stages of desperation. Yes, there is community in homelessness. In Kathleen Brehony's book, *Living a Connected Life*, she talks about the need to be connected as an important ingredient for mental health, no matter the economic status. We have a better chance of survival through community.

As we turned the corner in Honolulu we entered what the city calls the Kakaako neighborhood. This is where the homeless encampment is located. There were blocks of homeless…tent after tent after tent, housing probably 200+ people. And this didn't look temporary. These individuals and families had made these tents their homes. They had made a community for themselves. Their meager furniture was sure to have come from dumpsters. There were collections of cans and bottles to be taken to the recycle for cash, and dirty mattresses on the ground for sleep.

At yet another row of tents I saw a little girl's rusty pink bicycle and two children sitting in ragged lawn chairs looking at picture books. I caught my breath. Could this simply be a way of life for some? Kathryn had warned me that many of these tent dwellers had jobs and the children went to school. But with no subsidized housing for them, there was no place for them to go other than the streets.

In Honolulu, there are strict laws against living on the streets. They are regularly swept of all homeless possessions, which forces these individuals to shelters or to find other places, other sidewalks, to start over. And as a result, identification such as drivers' licenses are lost. Now the homeless are even more desperate than before. And they have to begin again in another location…find a tent…meet basic survival needs all over again, always with the knowledge that it is only a matter of time before their home will be swept away again.

Kathryn Xian is standing strongly and doing something about it. She's taking on the political system in Honolulu. Kathryn knows that the rights of the homeless are important. And she also knows that homelessness breeds sex trafficking, drug trafficking and more. Here's what she says, and the direction she is headed.

> "We need to both uphold justice and maintain democracy. With the recent criminalization of the houseless and passage of city ordinances eroding the basic civil rights of our neighbors in poverty, we have put democracy in the backseat and dangerously established the legal sanction of a class of people based on lack of income," said Kathryn Xian.
>
> To date, the City and County of Honolulu has spent more than $330,000 enforcing sidewalk nuisance regulations that went into effect last year, despite the recent recognition by federal courts that homeless people's property is protected by the Constitution's due process and the Fourth Amendment's privacy guarantees.
>
> "Between 2004 and 2008, the City of San Francisco spent $9.8 million on incarcerating the houseless, which succeeded only in wasting taxpayer dollars. These laws did not solve their houseless issues nor did it increase public safety. We must not follow their mistake. We need proven solutions to address poverty reduction, including raising the minimum wage, offering tax relief to low-income workers and families, and investing in public education," said Xian.

> *Xian also believes that the measure advances Hawaii's fight against human trafficking by affording homeless and runaway youth the rights needed to stave off exploitation.*
>
> "Many of our child survivors of trafficking are houseless youth. Criminalizing their vulnerability is not only immoral, but unconstitutional. Who will speak out for these children when the government proceeds with hurtful sweeps in blind persecution of their plight?" asked Xian. – Hawaii Reporter

MOMS AND CHILDREN - DOMESTIC VIOLENCE AND DEPRESSION

I've learned that the causes and reasons for homeless men, women and children are many. A homeless person can look just like you and me, can pass you on the street as a businessperson, can walk in and out of business buildings and places of work. It's because of the availability of homeless shelters that they can clean up and go out into the day, unnoticed. But they are still homeless. While the homeless population has more mental illness than the general population, most studies suggest that the majority of homeless are not mentally ill. Recent national estimates suggested 26 percent of the shelter population experienced mental illness. And what type of illness? Mostly depression.

Almost 40 percent of homeless people are substance abusers, according to *At Home on the Street* and today, approximately 671,859 Americans experience homelessness on any given night in the shelter system.

The profile of homeless people is, well, everyone. By that I mean single moms, working families, teenagers, the elderly, any of us!

The government has its plans and programs that seem to be

making a difference. Cities have their programs with dedicated locations that are granted for tent cities and shelters that are propped up with funds to stay open for the homeless and the needy. Federal homeless assistance programs address the need. But how do we end it? And how do we help homeless people be well and productive and proud of themselves in the long run? How do we help them have better futures?

Domestic violence is a catalyst to homelessness. It's often overlooked. But escaping violence is a leading cause of why women live on the streets. When women leave their homes, the cost of housing and the lack of a job or low wages and job availability keeps them homeless.

They sleep on couches, in cars, and on the floors of churches. Every day, hundreds of single moms and their children struggle to find shelter for the night and survive in San Francisco, which has one of the most expensive housing markets in the U.S.

> *A one-night count of the homeless in January 2015 at a shelter in San Francisco showed almost 7,500 adults, children and youth. But homeless rights advocates say single moms are an invisible, uncounted group because they usually sleep on couches of friends and family members or sleep in their cars before they are forced out on the street. - News Article by Halima Kazem,* The Guardian. *December 8, 2015.*

▼▼▼

▲▲▲

Lolly Galvin, at the young age of 25 "gets it." She understands that the homeless could be you or me. She knows that homelessness comes in many forms and at any time. She knew she wanted to dive in and learn the stories of the homeless, to use social media to create awareness and make a difference in her own way. What started as a small outreach turned into a month of living in a van and using the Internet for change.

We found her just in time to include her in this book.

▼▼▼

Lolly Galvin
SIT NEXT TO SOMEONE THAT OTHERS WALK BY

66 MY FIRST CHALLENGE WAS TO GET OVER THE SELF–DOUBT. 99

I started out simply. I wanted to use social media as a tool for good and positive changes. Slowly I began to share stories of homeless people I met while giving them necessities. People began to follow me and write me about how they could help homeless people in their cities and towns. The world is ultimately changed when people see their power to create healing in such simplistic ways.

My first challenge was to get over the self-doubt I had. When I started Dignity Project I had to put myself out there in both the "real" world and the social media world. It's odd at first, but slowly you begin to see how your actions can inspire others to do the same. At the very least, it might make someone rethink some old ideas. Since I had no formal plan, another challenge was figuring out what I was doing. Learning to trust myself and other people who helped me with each hurdle I faced.

I didn't have a background in non-profits or any specific extended work with the homeless. I honestly began by starting a gofundme.com page of $500.00 on Periscope for random acts of kindness. The goal was reached from complete strangers and my first act was to take a homeless man named Tom out to lunch and get to know him. I took a picture with Tom and shared his story. Tom changed my life for the better that day while touching other people. We never know the ways in which we will feel blessed when simply blessing others. There is such power in the human spirit.

LISTENING AND LEARNING

I continued to give essentials to homeless people while getting to know them through listening, learning and caring. That made me feel encouraged to share more stories with others through the platform of social media and before long my $500.00 grew to $2,000.00. I vowed that if my page hit $10,000 I would go live in a van for a month and give my time and resources to 14 other U.S. cities.

I met the goal. In fact, I surpassed it. And now I was about to have one of the most profound experiences of my life. The people I met had so many different stories, but at the root of their stories was often pain. It's easy to judge people when you don't let them share their experience. My passion lies in having people connect because that is how we realize how much more alike than different we are.

It's my belief that to many making a difference seems so far away or so much more unattainable than it is. So I attempt to show people that they can do exactly what I do. It doesn't take any special talent besides the desire to be present and sit next to someone that others walk by.

CONNECTING WITH DIGNITY

We all have the power to connect by showing others dignity. Many people feel uncomfortable extending a kind word or gesture but it is so needed in our world. People are isolated and hurting. What's inside of me is actually inside of all of us. It's the ability to choose by stepping out of our comfort zones and taking action.

Why is it so hard for us to see that we all matter? When we sit down with someone who has nothing and just share, it transcends the way we once thought. It opens our minds and our hearts to something greater than you or me.

What I have learned through the homeless is priceless. Many of these precious souls are not just smart but brilliant. Many have gifts that are perhaps suppressed for their shear need of survival. They have a different mentality and if you're willing to listen you cannot walk away without having learned something.

The Dignity Project is just a part of me now. The community of people that help keep it alive are absolutely amazing. My goal is to continue to do what I'm doing with an open mind and open heart. I want to learn and evolve while making my small difference in this world. For me, it's important to not be too rigid in your goal or plan, because ideas and creativity are fluid. Be open to whatever comes your way and don't fear it. All of it is meant to happen.

JUST START

Do It. Don't hesitate. Don't think too much. Forget about overanalyzing. There's always going to be a reason not to do something. The most commonly asked question I get is "where do I start?" The answer is, just start. Too many people get frozen in the thinking stage and never get to the action stage. The mind is a powerful thing. It can either hold you back or ignite your vision. Creating a movement doesn't take any special skill. It just takes dedication. Don't let it become overcomplicated because then it becomes this far off idea when its right inside you waiting to be released.

"The world is a mirror of your own beliefs." "If you believe that the world is a terrible place and people are terrible, that is what you will attract." "If you believe that the world is a kind place working together with you, you can attract whatever you want." "I see good everywhere simply because I look." "If you can see that and be that, things will change."

Lolly Galvin-Founder of The Dignity Project

▲▲▲

One Christmas season, I called the Julian Center, an organization assisting victims of domestic violence, and asked if my family could help a family in need. On one chilly December day in 1992, my children Jane, Catt and AJ and I set out to Walmart to buy toys, clothes, books—whatever we felt a young woman and her children would appreciate and need.

My kids kept loading the cart. I saw dollar signs. I already was buying their Christmas gifts, and with college expenses and my being a single mom, I had to watch my budget. But my cart kept filling up…and filling up…. The receipt totaled $300! I pulled out my credit card. *I'll pay it off*, I thought, the best Christmas present I could buy.

We spent all the next day wrapping our gifts. We loaded them up and headed for the shelter. My friends and family were worried. "That's a horrible place in the city. High crime. Are you sure you should drive there with your children? Please be careful."

I've never let fear stop me. My children don't let fear stop them. In my future was a ride across India with a driver who spoke no English, a time in a home in Kenya with victims of female genital mutilation, living in a tent with members of the Samburu tribe, swimming in the Ganges, living in an ashram and volunteering in an orphanage, traveling into the depths of Africa to support teen girls with sanitary towels so they can stay in school, and providing resources for women and children who had never seen an American; building a library for children in Costa Rica and houses for the homeless in the Dominican

Republic; working at a homeless shelter in Los Angeles, and so much more. Fear stops you from living your life. Fear stops you from the richness of making a difference. Fear holds you back.

It took the four of us all afternoon to wrap those presents, all the time talking about them, imagining the smiles on their faces when they would be opened. Maybe they would be the same as the smiles we had while wrapping them?

We brought our lovingly wrapped gifts to the private dwelling where the women and children were safe inside. We rang the bell and walked in, our family team fulfilling our mission of hope and love. The attendant took our packages and said thank you. Then we left. We had hoped to meet the family, to show them love— to put our arms around them. But safety for domestic violence victims and their children comes first. We understood. And we went home knowing that the gifts we gave to them meant as much to us as we felt they would mean to them.

I've learned more about homelessness since those times years ago with my children. And I've had my eyes opened to the many needs and my heart opened to the many stories of those who live it. One hundred million people are homeless worldwide.

Homelessness persists on a vast scale in both rich and poor countries because of economic and political disregard for the human rights of the poor according to Scott Leckie, director of the Centre on Housing Rights and Evictions in Geneva.

HOMELESSNESS IN RISHIKESH

I was walking through the streets of Rishikesh, India, where I had been staying at the Parmarth Niketan ashram. India is a country of many emotions. The people are beautiful and their smiles are captivating. In the midst of poverty, they have a spirit that lifts them up, in spite of their hardships. And it lifted me up, too. I was truly filled with a spirit of peace and joy while I was among these beautiful people.

This little village sits at the base of the Himalayan Mountains, perched beautifully at the edge of the Ganges River with its narrow streets, tiny shops and restaurants and many street merchants. It was a pensive and introspective time in my life. My mother had recently passed away after 12 long years with Alzheimer's. This trip was part of my healing, part of my seeing the world, and my future without my mother, through new eyes. My future came together in India. I met with a guru, prayed, and learned to meditate specifically for letting go of anger and fear from the past and forgiveness for myself and others.

I befriended a beautiful young mother and her two young children who were homeless on the streets where cows are sacred, beautiful Hindi music wafts through the air, and monks with their bald heads and orange robes walk in silence and peace. It is a crazy mix of all of humanity, this tiny village, where people come to bathe in the Ganges and become blessed. The power of the waters where in centuries past they floated their dead, prayed with floating candles adorned with flowers, and came together—all one. The floating candles ritual is still very much alive and I participated in prayer for my mother, my family and the world.

OUR FIRST CONNECTION WAS THROUGH HER YOUNG SON

I was sitting on a bench, thinking about the beauty of India and watching the people when he approached me and said, "Namaste." Even at his young age of probably three years old, he was already being taught to beg. He stole my heart. I looked around for a mother, and there she was, standing off in the distance with another child in her arms, watching us. I invited her to come over and sit with me.

Although I didn't speak Hindi and she didn't speak English, there was a connection between us, a sort of unspoken understanding between women. We know, yes, we know what is required of us. Regardless of being homeless or living in physical splendor or somewhere in between, with all the different roles we play, we have one very basic understanding of what it is to be female. Our stories are singular…but our passions are shared.

She didn't ask me for anything. We simply sat together, complete in the knowledge of the woman-ness between us. Understanding the responsibilities, the plight, the journeys, the strength and the weakness of what it means to be a woman. Our specific burdens and joys were different, that was understood, but our commonalities seemed to transcend that.

Eventually the baby cried and it was time to go—me back to the ashram and her back to the streets. We had sparked a friendship on some basic and visceral level. Now each time I ventured out from the ashram, on my way to help at the orphanage, walking through the streets I would see her. We would connect with a smile and a wave. We were friends. I would see her with her children along the Ganges. I would see her cleaning a dirty pot with mud and rinsing it with water, ready for the next time she could find food to make a meal. I would see her with her baby, sans diapers, and wrapped in a blanket for cover and warmth.

When my time in the ashram, my volunteering in the orphanage, and my personal meditative practice was over and I came back home, I've often thought of her. I did nothing for her. I was just her friend, in some odd way. A friend of a different culture, a different language, yet an understanding. Two women, two cultures. Two stories. Both with our own needs, yet a connection of sameness.

What could I have done for her? What can we do to help bring people out of homelessness, out of poverty, and out of hunger? Where do we begin? Where does it end?

▲▲▲

I learned about Shaaron Funderburk through the *Huffington Post* and I was touched by her story. I wanted her story in our book. Her story of abuse, homelessness and fighting her way back is a true example of a woman standing up for herself and her future. And eventually others. Shaaron took her difficult tragic childhood experiences and turned them into opportunities to change the world.

▼▼▼

Shaaron Funderburk
I AM A SURVIVOR

> **NO ONE TRIED TO FIND OUT WHY I HAD BLACK EYES, CHOKE MARKS AROUND MY NECK, A BUSTED LIP AND BRUISED RIBS.**

I am Shaaron M. Funderburk. I am a survivor of my emotions, coming from a horrific past. I struggle from emotional, physical and mental damage. At the age of 11 my world changed. I went from being an innocent little girl to having my choices taken away. Most people are given a chance to give their virginity away; mine was taken by four neighborhood boys. These boys were a year or two older than myself. There was this game that was played called "hide and go get it." I hated the game and never wanted to play it. At dusk I always headed home because I knew the older kids in the neighborhood were going to play this game. Instead of letting me go home, they would chase me and carry me to the woods. The rapes were different every time and lasted all summer. And, this is when the horror began.

As I aged, the little girl inside me never grew up. You see, every feeling after that led to the 11-year-old and the damage.

When I turned 15, I was angry and began to rebel and act out in school. When I would get in trouble, my only escape was anger. So I fought, I lied, I hurt others—all because I had no coping skills and no one who would listen. I was always told, "You are just a bad child."

Teachers would tell me I was dumb, stupid and unable to learn. No one tried to find out why I had black eyes, choke marks around my neck, a busted lip and bruised ribs. I made it through school because my mother only wanted one thing—a high school diploma. My emotional damage came from teachers because I had these behaviors and couldn't explain. No one would try to deal with me. They would pass me through school with barely passing grades, just to get rid of me.

I BELIEVED WHAT THEY WERE SAYING

When I think back, I realize they couldn't help me. This is where the mental damage came from. Being told you will never amount to anything by teachers and family members, I didn't strive—I didn't try. I believed what they were saying. Looking for love in all the wrong places, I slept with anybody who showed me any kind of attention. It wasn't hard to start selling myself. The first time I made money was performing oral sex and I didn't do it right. He paid me and then he beat me. But because of all the abuse from childhood, I didn't know the difference. I thought it was normal to be beaten after sex. And these behaviors went on for years. I sold myself for $10 or $15 until I started using crack cocaine. I learned the streets. I got good at what I was doing. The street life became my way of life. I could hustle better than I could read. I could make money, but I couldn't keep a job.

As the drugs took over, I became homeless and slept with men to support myself. By this time, I didn't like me, so I didn't like others. I was hanging around with anybody who had the objective to make money: stealing, robbing and rolling people just for drugs. I went without bathing, sometimes weeks at a time. Shame, dereliction, degradation, isolation—all of these feelings and emotions began to take over the management of my life. But I couldn't stop.

HITTING ROCK BOTTOM

I remember the specific date I hit rock bottom. It was May 18, 1994. I began my journey to getting and staying clean the next day. I was tired of being a nothing and a nobody. I was alone in the struggle to become clean and sober. My family didn't know how to help me and I was in failed relationship after failed relationship. I had been making bad choices, had no life skills and I was just plain lost. There was no place like Off the Streets for me to find refuge, comfort and help. Once I got clean and sober, I reached out to help others and it grew from there.

I know what it is like to wake up and not know what has happened in your life for a period of time because you were "cracked" out of your mind and your best friend is a crack pipe. I also know firsthand what it is like to be locked up behind bars and see the tears in your mother's eyes as she pleads with you to change. One day as I took a good look at myself, I realized that I had hit bottom and I said, "This is it. I've had enough and I cannot go on living this way. I have got to change for the better." And change, I did. Not only did I change, now I help others to change.

I ADVOCATE FOR WOMEN IN TROUBLE

I have become a modern-day "Sojourner Truth" to any addict or person who has lost hope in themselves due to substance abuse or a life behind bars. As the founder of Off the Streets Program, Inc., which I started with my personal funds, I have been reaching out to help countless other women who wander the streets of Gastonia, NC, and surrounding areas. My success is with women who are dealing with rape, molestation, abandonment, unhealthy relationships, depression, physical, mental and emotional abuse, and low self-esteem or no self-esteem. On any given day, my team and I can be found walking the streets of Gaston and surrounding areas seeking women who have turned to the streets. I have put together a team that has the know-how to beat the disease of addiction. This program is for addicts and is run by former addicts. I am also known to frequently visit within the courts, jail system and detox centers as I advocate for women in trouble.

Because of the success of the program and the help I have given women, I have had to face pimps and drug dealers. They have threatened and lied to me to keep their women from getting out of the lifestyle. I have had false warrants, character assassination and arrests on my journey. I faced it like the woman I have become. I turned myself in, because I had done nothing wrong in my endeavor to save a young lady's life. With the character assassination, I continue to stay focused, no matter what comes at me. I believe in what I am doing and so I let my character speak for itself. I have gone to court only to see the men get laughed at by stating in front of the judge, the police officers and the whole courtroom, that they are afraid of me because I am a strong woman. You see, I live in a small town and my name is known in this community. I have been doing this for 20 years.

Off the Streets helps women with addiction, who are being released from incarceration or who are living on the street, to overcome their addictions. The 700 or more ladies of Off the Streets have faced, traced and erased innumerable amounts of obstacles. Because of the program, they regained self-respect, self-worth and pride. These women found the courage to take their place in society, becoming productive members of society and providing strength for one another. Off the Streets is a family. They reconcile with their families; the women regain custody of their children. These women are going from walking the streets and being on drugs to becoming mothers, wives and college graduates.

One hundred percent of the women have found gainful

employment. They have learned to feel good about who they are and what they are doing. Some of the women have started their own businesses or have become managers at their place of employment. Off the Streets has helped women to open such businesses as painting and construction, dog grooming and landscaping. These women created their business after felony convictions made it hard to find work. Women have regained their professional certifications and licenses to practice in their chosen field.

STOP BEING VICTIMS, AND START BEING SURVIVORS!

If I ever had a podium and a voice to speak to the whole world, I would say, "Women, stop being victims and start being survivors. You are still here, so there is purpose in your pain. You see, God had to take me all the way into what he wanted to use me for. I can tell every woman I encounter that I have some measure of identifying. I know pain. I know low self-esteem. I know inadequacy. I know damage. So women, it is okay to look back, but you never have to go back. Stop allowing your childhood to dictate your adulthood. You can take adulthood and protect all the pain from your childhood."

You see, everything I went through is not wasted. When I sit down to do intakes to put women in my house, I tell them my story. Immediately, they feel that they are not alone and that there just might be some help for them after all.

Shaaron Funderburk–Founder of Off the Streets Program, Inc.

▲▲▲

LOVE IN THE DOMINICAN REPUBLIC

It was finally happening. It was the day we were boarding the plane headed to the Dominican Republic—San Pedro, to be exact, to build homes for three homeless families. Forty-eight adults and six children from different parts of the U.S. came together to withstand the heat, to hammer, saw, paint, love and laugh—to build homes and hope for these families.

For some, this was their first time to an impoverished area like San Pedro. Not only were we helping by building homes, but the people and the culture were opening the eyes of many of us.

My son, AJ, had built homes here before and was our project leader. He had experienced the work of Homes for Hope and YWAM (Youth With A Mission). And thanks to a private donor, we were all able to go.

We filled three buses with excited volunteers early on our first morning. When we arrived at the neighborhood we were ready to get started. Some of the families on the dirt streets lived in corrugated aluminum structures, a few were cinder block, and many looked like there was a start to a home that was never completed. Yet it was obvious which homes had been erected by volunteers and project leaders for YWAM. They were all about 400 square feet and painted bright yellow with blue trim, and they sat on a slab of concrete. Inside those little houses there were families, there was self-respect and there was a fresh start.

We were anxious to meet the three families who were waiting to work alongside us to build their new home.

We arrived at our location. The old houses had been torn down and the families greeted us! Many smiles, many hugs, many thank you's…and we hadn't even begun. It was an event: all the neighborhood turned out. And for those three days that we built the homes, the families worked with us…children with paint brushes, men with saws, putting on roofs in the heat of the day. Inside, outside, getting closer to a new life.

One house went to Ernestine, a single mom with two children. She had an empty lot that was soon to be filled with her own home! Ernestine's plan was to use her home as a place to run her business as a beautician once she could raise the school fees and complete the classes.

One house went to Juan and his wife, two children and two grandchildren. They had been living in an 8x10 corrugated aluminum box. Juan had recently had heart bypass surgery and his wife was ill. No one had a job. Every day, Juan helped the volunteer team with the build. Hungry and weak and still recovering, he insisted on being a part of creating this house for his family. He understood the magnitude of the day.

And finally, Jose and Maria, who watched from across the street as our volunteers swooped in and got started. Their two grandchildren played with the children of the families that had come with us, finding their own connection as children from two different worlds.

The process of building a house is much like building a life. The foundation holds it all together. The construction takes time. It can be done quickly with no real direction or strategy, or it can be done carefully, thoughtfully, and made to last. The direction this project took those three families truly gave them a new foundation.

So many women are using their voices and leading the way to create awareness and stand up against homelessness.

Robin Emmons and Pat LaMarche are two of them.

SOWING GOOD

I was first aware of Robin Emmons and her work one Saturday night two years ago when I was watching CNN's annual "Heroes" event. I loved her energy; I loved her cause. I knew I had to meet her. And I did. She was invited to speak about her work, Sow Much Good, at our annual fundraiser.

After spending 20 years in corporate America, a force tugged inside Robin Emmons to leave her job in the financial services industry for an unplanned journey. One week after quitting, Emmons helped her brother find residence in a mental health facility; however, while being treated, he became unhealthy due to the consumption of canned and sugary foods. Robin, a gardener, donated produce to the facility and her brother's physical health improved dramatically.

In her TED Talk, Robin suggests that our God-given humanity is an inalienable right. And that includes rights of the homeless. She says that sometimes we become apathetic because we are overwhelmed by the issue of homelessness. And it IS overwhelming.

"I can't tell you what it feels like when I'm driving to a corporate office on a rainy morning and I see my brother at a bus stop wearing a trash bag to keep warm." She can't describe the horror of hearing on the news that a homeless person froze to death under the freeway and she spends her entire weekend calling the police, the morgue and service agencies to see if it was her loved one.

So Robin uses food as a vehicle to promote social justice on important issues like homelessness. She started small by digging up her entire backyard and sowing the seeds for the nonprofit, Sow Much Good. She dedicated herself to eliminating systemic barriers in the food system that disproportionately affect the working poor and underserved populations.

And the rest is history.

LIVING ON THE MARGIN

Pat LaMarche was a candidate for Vice President for the Green Party of the United States in the 2004 election. She realized that her chances for winning an election, even though she and her running mate, David Cobb, had much to bring to the campaign, were slim. But she came to understand that she could give a voice to the millions of Americans who are homeless and are not heard.

Pat began her 14-day journey of living in homeless shelters across the country and utilized the media to create awareness and ask for solutions. Her insightful book, *Left Out in America*, introduced the world to the intensity of the problem, a firsthand look at the realities of shelter life and street life, and the faces of many she met along the way. At times, the shelters were full and her place for the night was on the street, in an alleyway or an entry to a building. On one of these nights it was cold. Here's a piece from her book:

> *Nestled in the elbow of a building, where the outer wall turned a corner, was a patch of loose soil…a perfect location. Turns out that soft earth makes a much better mattress than concrete.*
>
> *It occurred to me that I had the only sleeping bag. I apologized that it wouldn't keep anyone warm but it might keep us dry. Ron said, "Haven't you heard of a 'homeless blanket'? Nobody gets to be shy when it's cold."*
>
> *He lay down next to me and put his arms around me and said, "Come on everybody, let's keep her warm." Then the other kids all came and lay down with us. We all hung onto each other. They all took turns telling what their lives had been like. Why they ended up on the street. Who they knew that got off the street and who died there. Some spoke of things that were unspeakable. Every one of them had a memory that would have been better forgotten.*

▲▲▲

Caroline Barnett is the epitome of grace, generosity and love. The work she has done as the cofounder of the Dream Center in Los Angeles impacts 80,000 families and individuals each month.

Their reach is wide, yet almost everything they do centers around homelessness in some form. From mobile hunger relief to transitional housing, to a shelter for victims of trafficking, and more, her volunteer-based organization has developed into 100 Dream Centers nationally and internationally.

Here's an excerpt from her book, *Willing to Walk on Water: Step Out in Faith and Let God Work Miracles through Your Life*, as she tells the story of her trigger moments for feeding the homeless.

▼▼▼

Caroline Barnett
THE HUNGER OF HOMELESSNESS

> ❝ CHILDREN LIVE HERE, I GRIEVED TO MYSELF, LITTLE CHILDREN. THIS SHOULD NOT BE HAPPENING. NOT IN THE RICHEST COUNTRY IN THE WORLD. ❞

It was a spring day in 1997 and I was helping out in the Dream Center reception office when the phone rang. A social worker on the other end told me about a family in need living only a few blocks away from us. I thanked her, then called my best friend from Sweden, Sara, who had recently flown in to volunteer at the Dream Center for a year, and asked her to meet me at the campus food pantry. Together we packed and bagged bread, fresh produce, and some canned goods into three boxes, loaded them into my 1978 diesel Volvo station wagon, and headed to the address the social worker had given me.

I drove slowly down the street, passing one dilapidated apartment building after another. They had broken windows and cracked siding, and their roofs looked on the verge of collapsing, every one of them in need of repair. Lawns were littered with broken beer bottles, mounds of dog feces, and half-eaten *elotes* (corn on the cob in the husk sold from nearby street carts). There were no grassy areas for the kids to play on, just random patches of crumbling cement and dead plants in unattended containers. From one apartment, the music blared so loudly you could hear it down the entire street. Every time I saw such an impoverished neighborhood, it broke my heart, but it wasn't as shocking to me as it was to my friend.

Finally, we arrived. When I knocked on the door, it opened with a loud creaking sound. There stood a weary mother, smiling faintly. My heart tumbled as I quickly counted eight children clothed only in underwear or diapers huddled around her, their eyes wide and curious. The smell from inside the room hit me full force–sweaty bodies and unchanged diapers. I sensed it had been a long time since anyone had had a bath. As tired and ragged as the woman looked, she couldn't have been much older than 25.

Once the kids spotted the boxes of food we carried, a few of them gasped in amazement, some even leapt into our arms, practically knocking us over. I accidentally dropped one of the bags in the commotion, and a handful of produce plummeted to the floor. One of the children grabbed a zucchini that was rolling down the dirt-covered hallway and excitedly shoved it in her mouth, taking noisy bites with her brown-stained teeth.

A raw zucchini? I thought. Many kids refuse to eat cooked vegetables at all, no matter how tasty, and this little girl is devouring one with hardly any taste at all! How long has it been since they've had anything to eat?

The apartment was practically bare, with linoleum floors that were cracked and filthy. The foam stuffing was coming out of the couch cushions that littered the living room. My guess was that the cushions doubled as the children's beds. The only things in the kitchen cupboards were dead bugs. *Children live here*, I grieved to myself, *little children. This should not be happening. Not in the richest country in the world.*

All eight kids followed and surrounded us, so close on our heels it was hard not to trip over or bump into them. They clamored around us, 16 outstretched arms desperately grabbing at anything we tried to put on the shelves. It was a madhouse. I felt fingers gripping and shaking my arms, trying to knock a loaf of bread out of my hand. These kids were hungry. Only God knew the last time they had had a proper meal.

MY TRIGGER

What I saw that day changed my life. It was my trigger, one that created in me a passion to make a change and take action. I walked away from that apartment knowing I couldn't sit back and do nothing about the hunger problem that ravaged impoverished families and children.

I did have a foundation to build upon—the Dream Center's food bank. It had been one of the fit ministries created to meet an immediate need. We originally opened the food bank on campus to the public on certain days. The need was so great, however, that people would show up on any day of the week asking for food. We never turned anyone away and would serve whoever came, but also let them know to come back at particular times.

The ministry was providing a vital service, but I realized we could turn something good into something great. A large percentage of the people who needed food had no way to get to the food bank. They didn't have cars or money for public transportation. If we were going to maximize our ministry, we needed to get to the people who couldn't get to us. We needed to be proactive and meet them where they lived, not merely serve those who showed up on our doorstep. God was beginning to unfold a plan in my mind: a mobile food-bank ministry.

With the heartbreaking scene at the apartment still fresh in my mind, I sat down with Pastor Matthew and described what I had seen. He gave me the green light to start a mobile food-bank ministry. (I called my future husband Pastor Matthew before we started dating and even during the beginning of our courtship. I figured if our relationship didn't work out, it would make it easier to switch back to calling him Pastor.)

After receiving the go-ahead, I paused to reflect on how God works. A few months earlier, I would have laughed at even considering the idea, let alone spearheading it. It wasn't something that interested me. Oh, I recognized that hunger is a severe problem worldwide. I had grown up watching hundreds of television spots showing starving kids in third-world countries with bulging bellies and vacant eyes. Though the images moved me to tears, they never propelled me toward action. I would simply change the channel or turn off the TV.

My outlook shifted, however, when I stood in the midst of eight emaciated children in my neighborhood, begging for a cracker, a chip, a raw vegetable, or a piece of fruit—anything to curb the hunger pangs that throbbed in their bellies. They were my trigger.

What about you? What injustice grips your heart the most? Is it crack babies, orphaned toddlers whose lives have been confined to cribs, AIDS victims who can't afford treatment, children whose innocence has been stolen by sex traffickers? Maybe it's a single mother you've met who barely sees her children because she is working three jobs and still struggles to pay the bills. Being sympathetic shows you have a heart. But having sympathy and taking a step forward to effect change are two different things. When you are triggered by a particular injustice, your compassion doesn't end with a few shed tears. It leads to action.

God has made each one of us unique. I believe that's why our hearts break over different causes. I may feel a pull toward helping orphans in the foster-care system, while you feel motivated to be an advocate for the homeless in your community. Whether your passion is drug-addicted youth, providing clean water for a village in a third-world country, or teaching adults how to read, God has placed a unique area of compassion within your heart to be sparked and set aflame.

Caroline Barnett-Founder of The Dream Center and the author of *Willing to Walk on Water: Step Out in Faith and Let God Work Miracles through Your Life*

▲▲▲

I would venture to guess that when we think of the homeless, we typically don't think of the children and teens. We don't know accurate statistics, because it's a hidden population. Each year millions of kids and teens sleep in a place they can't call home. For some, their bed is in a shelter. For others, it's in a car or on the street. Homelessness for children and teenagers can have physical and mental effects that can last for years to come. "Homelessness is a traumatic experience for people, because they lose everything. They lose their routines, privacy, friends and pets," says Dr. Ellen Bassuk, associate professor of psychiatry at Harvard Medical School and founder of The National Center for Homelessness (in an article by Shawn Radcliffe from *Healthline News*). "They're in situations where they don't know where the next meal is going to come from, or where they're going to be tomorrow," she says. She notes that if you walk into a public school classroom, one of those students is going to become homeless or is currently homeless.

Researching homelessness I learned from *Psychology Today* that, "Approximately one-third of the United States' homeless population are youth."

The situation may be much larger than we realize, too, as it's hard to track youth. They stay at friends' houses, move from couch to couch with single moms, bunk in with relatives on the short term or even move from one city to the next as the seasons change.

It's hard to point out homeless youth. They may be relatively well-dressed and in many ways are doing their best to hold onto the small routines that people with stable housing may take for granted. They are not "classically homeless," but instead can be going to school, yet sleeping in homeless shelters at night or living in tent cities with working parents, as is often the case in Honolulu and all over the tent city population.

"People walk past the homeless all the time in their lives. A lot of homeless youth are visible, but invisible," says Dr. Niranjan S. Kamik, Rush University Medical Center.

Jan Stone, wrote the book *Absence of Tears: A Collection of True Short Stories of Homeless Women and Children*. Jan has lived her life giving back. As a compassionate human being, volunteer and champion of the needy, she was inspired to develop a program for incarcerated fathers who were being reintroduced to society in Las Vegas. She worked with the Star Program, which was one of the country's first day care facilities for disabled adults; and her eventual work after retirement at a homeless shelter produced the stories in this book.

After her death in 2008, Jan's son Timothy Stone found a folder with the original draft. A collection of stories about and for the women and children she met in the shelter sheds light on what it is like to be homeless, the shame some felt and the dreams they hold onto….

The following stories are about a teen girl and a young child who lived in the shelter.

THE SECRET

She didn't tell anyone she lived in a homeless shelter. She didn't want anyone to know.

If she had to give an address, she gave the shelter's post office box number. When friends wanted to walk her home, she declined or made some excuse. If she had to arrange a meeting with someone, she met them at the local convenience store or at the nearest mall. She made up elaborate stories as to why she couldn't invite anyone to her place.

At the shelter she was known as a friendly person and often helped with the small children. She played games and read aloud and helped with school kids' homework. She made the morning coffee even though she didn't drink any herself. She often scrubbed the bathroom floor as her shelter chore. She was careful to obey the rules and never rocked the boat.

About four o'clock each afternoon, she found a table and sat writing for a long time.

When she left the shelter, she always opened the door and peered both ways to make sure no one was passing by. Preserving her secret was important, and she used elaborate means.

She didn't care if she had the right logo on her clothing, but she did care that no one knew she lived in a homeless shelter.

She was a teenager, the shelter was her secret, and it was important that it be kept a secret.

THE FIRST SNOWFALL

It was the wish of a homeless child.

Her name was Sarah and she was nine years old. Her wish was made while blowing out the candles on the April birthday cake at the shelter. Once a month the shelter had a birthday cake to honor all who were born in the month. Sarah was an April child, and after she helped blow out the candles, I asked her what she had wished for. Of course, I expected her to tell me her wish would not come true if she put it into words, but it didn't happen that way. She was happy to share that she had wished she could wake up one morning and find everything covered with snow. Snow? Why snow?

Sarah told me it had to do with a magical moment, and I found that a snowfall sits in a young mind in the same compartment as ribbons on presents, the first ice cream cone, and a soft, familiar blanket. To wake up to a world covered with white is to wake up to awe and wonder. Everything is changed. Every tree, every sidewalk, every car, every roof is fluffy and perfect. There is no dirt, no darkness, no ugliness.

Sarah very much wanted a world with brightness and light.

She and her mother came to the shelter late one night, eyes fearful, glances backward, and terror enveloping them like a blanket. Their clothes had logos on the pockets and their shoes bore well-known names, but they were empty-handed. They had left with nothing.

They stayed only a few days, but in that time came the birthday celebration and the wish for snow. Most of us would have foresworn any wishes we might have for the rest of our lives to guarantee a bright white world for Sarah.

How many candles must we blow out? How many wishbones must we break? How many shooting stars must we see? It is, after all, only a wish from a homeless child. What does she know about the first snowfall, and how can it possibly matter to the world around her?

HOMELESSNESS HAS MANY CAUSES

Not all homelessness is from a lack of work: it can happen naturally. Natural disasters wreak havoc on our world and with them comes loss of property, homes, belongings and keepsakes.

After disasters strike, the immediate needs are met by doctors and nurses—the medical community comes together. Then it's the places to stay: churches, shelters, homes of others, makeshift structures and more. It does indeed take a village.

▲▲▲

Meet Marie Griffin. When Hurricane Katrina hit in 2005 she knew she had to do something. And she did. Understanding that children are victims of homelessness, too, she put her heart and her resources into a project of love at just the right moment. With a little help from Santa's elves...

▼▼▼

Marie Griffin

SANTA KNOWS WHERE YOU ARE SLEEPING

❝ WHAT CHRISTMAS GIFT COULD POSSIBLY BE GREATER THAN A **BEAMING SMILE FROM A CHILD** AND THAT OF HIS OR HER STUNNED, THANKFUL PARENTS... ❞

Every Christmas Eve for the past 20+ years, my sister Bunky has been Santa Claus. With her mastery of theatrical makeup, plus some strategically placed pillows, she's so convincing that our nephews Eric and Stephen still believed in Santa Claus much longer than most children. They had no idea that Bunky was Santa Claus all those years. When Bunky finally told them, their reaction was, "Wow, you love us so much!"

Bunk and I would make the 1.5-hour car trip every Christmas Eve to our sister Rosemary's home. Santa Claus would climb up on their roof and walk around ringing her reindeer bells, saying, "Ho ho ho!" in her deepest voice, causing Eric and Stephen to wake up. They'd run to the staircase to peer through the banister to watch Santa put their gifts under the tree, take a cookie for himself and carrots for his reindeers, before heading out with a deep-voiced, "Merry Christmas!" It was pure magic, the true wonder of the season.

I was Santa's driver and helper. Our nephews were so mesmerized by Santa, they never knew that I was watching from the dining room every year, having entered from the back of the house where Rosemary would have chocolate chip cookies fresh out of the oven waiting for us. The night was still young after this fantastic appearance, so Bunk and I would share Santa's love. At first, we stopped by friends' houses, but soon after, we added hospitals. Bunk is also the Easter Bunny. We've made appearances at homeless and domestic abuse shelters as the Easter Bunny, too, but that's a whole different story.

SANTA MEETS KATRINA

Hurricane Katrina hit right before New York Fashion Week. Bunk and I both have worked Fashion Week every season for years. It's one of the busiest weeks in the year for us. Designer Carolina Herrera has long said, "Fashion is a dream, a fantasy." By day, Bunk and I were living that dream. The most beautiful models in the world strode down the runway in exquisite collections while photographers' camera flashes lit up the tents and celebrities in the front row gave standing ovations to designers taking their closing bows.

The nightmare came at night when we walked in the door and turned on CNN. Every night during Fashion Week, I'd sit in front of the television and tears would just pour down my face. I knew that we had to do something to help, so I emailed my friend Jason Carroll, CNN National Correspondent. I told him we wanted to come down the second Fashion Week was over. He replied that there was no power, no water, and that he and the crew were living in a trailer, eating granola bars. That wouldn't have stopped us, but I knew we needed a plan before we went down, to ensure we were truly a help and not a hindrance during this epic natural disaster.

The people of New Orleans desperately needed emotional

relief, something familiar, normalcy. They needed hope and some joy. That's how Santa Knows Where You're Sleeping (SKWYAS) came to be. Bunky is a genius at names, and this name said it in a nutshell. Our mission was simple: SKWYAS was created as an initiative dedicated to keeping the magic of Christmas alive for children displaced from their homes. No matter where you are, Santa will find you.

It was time to call Jason now that our plan was hatched. We needed to know if any elementary schools were open and operating. Jason connected us to Sr. Mary Rose, the principal of Cathedral Academy. We told her our plan and it was a go for Santa Claus to make a surprise appearance at the school on November 11.

Bunk and I drafted a letter to our family and friends asking if they wanted to participate in SKWYAS. We would send participants a Santa letter from a child, but they had to agree to gift the child with exactly what they asked for. This way, they'd know that Santa really heard them, saw them, understood them, and loved them.

A JOYFUL RESPONSE

On the afternoon of November 6, I hit "send" on my computer. Off went our letter and out I went to walk my dog. In the short time I was walking Herbie, my computer crashed since so many people wanted to be part of SKWYAS. I cried with joy.

Bunk and I flew down to New Orleans on November 10. We were the only civilians on the plane. All the other passengers were NYC firefighters coming to help their New Orleans brothers and sisters. Even as we arrived in the pitch darkness, we could see the chaos Katrina left in her wake. Our cab wove around boats on their sides in the middle of the streets.

First thing in the morning, Sr. Mary Rose pulled up in the convent's minivan. Sr. Mary Rose was cast right out of a movie. Young, fun, compassionate and eternally optimistic, she was literally a Godsend to her students.

As the children lined up in the playground, they had no idea of the surprise that awaited them. Santa's introduction by Sr. Mary Rose was met with great excitement. The letter writing officially began for the entire school. Young children sat on Santa's lap and whispered their wishes in Bunk's ear. I wrote the letters for them. With my long, blonde hair, they all thought I was Santa's daughter. Santa later visited the older children in their classrooms to pick up their letters and put them in his sack, the same one we used for years with Eric and Stephen.

Word got out that Santa was in town, and we visited two additional Catholic schools that day. When the day was over, we exhaustedly boarded the plane with close to 1,200 letters in Santa's sack. Part 1 of our mission was accomplished. Part 2 was matching the children's letters with the very best participants, based on the gifts they were requesting. Everyone from Brownie troops to celebrities took part in our heartfelt initiative. The magic resided in the right fit.

One boy wanted a Bible. We knew that our mother was the perfect fit with him. A girl described her dream doll, one that was particularly colorful and custom-made. A fashion designer was perfectly matched with her letter. Yet another child asked for a chocolate fountain. A foodie was her ideal match. When a boy asked for a blue guitar, Bunk made his dream come true.

Wishes truly tugged at our hearts. Some children requested gifts not for themselves, but for people they loved. When a boy asked for roses for his grandmother, he got them. This is what our friends and family most warmly recall about SKWYAS. It was the most personal, intimate and sweet initiative they had ever been part of. Magic and wonder were in these small, yet very important, details.

Initiative they had never been part of. Magic and wonder were in these small, yet very important, details.

When we ran out of children's letters to distribute, we expanded SKWYAS to the Junior League of Mobile, Alabama, where generous participants sent gifts for an additional 1,800 children.

Sr. Mary Rose was the keeper of the boxes sent. We did this for two reasons. Sr. and her sisters kept us abreast of the deliveries, so we knew that every child's box was received. Additionally, we wanted to keep the magic of Christmas alive for parents. Parents picked up their children's packages so they could keep their family's holiday traditions intact during a time of unimaginable upheaval. It was our way of delivering hope to them, as well as helping them maintain their pride.

The media wanted to film us distributing the packages. We passed. This was a private, tender moment for families, not a press opportunity for us. It gave Bunk and me great joy knowing that more than 3,000 presents were being opened that Christmas Eve and Christmas morning.

SANTA FINDS KIBERA

A year later, CNN entered once again. I was watching Christiane Amanpour's special, called, "Where Have All The Parents Gone?" which told the story of Kenyan children orphaned by AIDS living at the Stara Rescue Center in Kibera, the Kenyan slum infamous for its overcrowding, poverty and lack of sanitation. Christiane connected us with Josephine Mumo, the founder of the center. SKWYAS went global.

The 470 letters from Africa were not nearly as colorful and childlike as the New Orleans letters. They were all written in pencil with the word ORPHAN written on top. Heartbreaking. Children requested clothes and blankets.

No toys. Our friends and family quickly requested letters once again. We were overwhelmed by their continued love, support and generosity. SKWYAS Kibera was a much larger financial commitment for the participants due to the international shipping fees, but it was as wildly successful as SKWYAS New Orleans.

WE JUST NEED TO KNOW WHAT TO DO

What I do know for sure after these two life-altering experiences: people truly want to help. They just need to know how. Tell them exactly what you need. Just keep it very simple, and success will be guaranteed. Years later, people still speak of SKWYAS with great sentiment.

Secondly, just do it. Whether it's a big initiative like SKWYAS or something much smaller, do whatever you can to make a difference in a child's life. Head down to your local post office during the holidays, pick a letter to Santa and create magic and wonder for a child. Bunk and I pick a handful of letters every Christmas. I still drive Santa around on Christmas Eve until the sun comes up.

What Christmas gift could possibly be greater than a beaming smile from a child and that of his or her stunned, thankful parents when Santa Claus appears at their door on Christmas Eve? Everyone believes in Santa Claus—and love—during Christmastime, most especially Bunk and I.

Marie Griffin - President of Griffin Marketing & PR

WHAT CAN YOU DO:

1. Volunteer with an organization fighting homelessness.

2. Learn more and use social media to create awareness.

3. Treat the homeless with respect.

4. Donate to a charity that helps the homeless.

5. Get involved with local government for affordable housing.

Section 4 – Education

❝ IF YOU TEACH A MAN TO FISH HE'LL EAT FOR A LIFETIME. IF YOU TEACH A WOMAN TO FISH SHE'LL FEED THE WHOLE VILLAGE. ❞

Hillary Clinton

▲▲▲

I had certainly been told the story of teaching a man to fish. I remember the first time my father explained it to me; I was maybe five years old. And it stuck. In fact, I'm just now thinking as I write that it could have been that moment with my father that brought me to my life's work.

There are all kinds of choices when it comes to how you live your life. You just need to recognize them and take the steps, however small, toward claiming them. And education, which gives you the tools and the impetus to make your own stand in the world, can help you get there.

It took many moves from town to town, home to home, school to school until our family finally landed in Indiana for me to understand that there is always change, and embracing it makes your life richer. And it took my mother, who believed in education and told us every day we would go to college, we would make our way in the world. She treasured education and understood its power. She'd fought for hers. At 15 years old she moved from the family farm to a small town in rural Illinois where the nearest high school was located. She lived with a family; room and board were exchanged for cooking and cleaning. It was her chance to continue her high school education.

So it was never a question for my sisters and me that we had the right to an education. It was never considered that we wouldn't graduate from high school and go on to an advanced education. It was part of an accepted future. I can still see the little glass piggy bank on my dresser that my parents reminded me was the place to drop pennies in to save for college. That bank symbolized my future and the collection of pennies was placed lovingly by the small hand of a little girl, me, with wonder about what her grown-up self would be and the path my education would take me on.

But what many girls that age didn't learn, just like me, was that our role in education was still very limited because we were girls. Our choices were limited. In this big vast world of opportunity that we lived in, we were counseled that there were careers for girls and other careers for boys.

Years ago I heard an interview with Marlo Thomas. It was 1972, when she was promoting her book, *Free to Be You and Me*. She said, "Nobody asks a man if he wants to be a daddy or a doctor." Yet the same wasn't true at this time for women. That was a hallmark book that developed into a television show for children and is as relevant today as it was those many years ago. If you don't know it, you should. You can still find it on Amazon.

By 1972 I was a mother and a college student. Girls in my high school were often married right after graduation. When I think back on those times I think of the movie *Peggy Sue Got Married*. It took place in the '50s. Like her, I lived in a small town, with one high school; everyone knew everyone, my boyfriend was the captain of the football team and I was the cheerleader. Just like Peggy Sue.

The beginnings of the women's movement were happening right about the time I was in college. By my sophomore year I was married, and my junior year I was a mother. I did recognize my opportunities. I just decided they should all happen at the same time. Motherhood, college education, marriage… ouch! All by the time I was 21. I had to grow up fast. And I was determined to have it all. But still there was something missing…and that something was the right to be anything I wanted to be. It wasn't anyone's fault that I was limited in my choices for a career. It was just simply the way it was in the 70s. Millions of women were struggling along with me. Some of them bonded together and started speaking up. I hadn't met them yet. I hadn't met women like me, yet.

I didn't question the direction I was headed, but there was an uneasy, unidentifiable tug on my heart that there were supposed to be greater things. Something more for my own life. And I knew I'd find it through my education. I can still see my mother's face when she told me school is the key to my future. But what future? I had to find that out on my own over years of living and learning. And still today, when I want to start something new, or challenge my current situation or thoughts, it's education—through reading, listening, and learning, to find my answers.

Fast-forward many years to the beginning of the Women Like Us Foundation. I am a lifelong feminist and believer in the power that women have to change the world. I had worked most of my adult life as an entrepreneur and made life decisions that felt right for me. I understood all along the consequences that could come from them. And when I finally landed in the philanthropic world, the world of speaking out for the vulnerable, seeing need and helping women sustain their own charitable work and leadership, I had found my way home.

I'm in good company. Shirley Osborne, CEO of Posh Affairs, Inc., (a women's services group encompassing Feminine Alchemy, which brings together accomplished and engaging women for discussion and collaborations such as The Girls Education Project, a nonprofit mentoring young girls), is a contributor in the book, *Leading Women*. Shirley talks about the importance of women bringing other women along. She states that:

"We must actively seek the elimination of the disparities and injustices that hold women back, and which as a direct consequence, restrict the well-being of our families and hinder the development of our societies. The philanthropy that has been, and will continue to be, vital to women's continued empowerment can be conducted in any of a million different ways. However, it is my submission that the best, most sustainable forms of philanthropy that will have the biggest, most enduring impact are to give women information, to facilitate their access to sources of information, and to support them in acquiring the skills with which to utilize and benefit from information. History bears this out."

EDUCATION EQUALS EMPOWERMENT

We all know that education is key to a quality of life that keeps the basics in line. With education, we can all get better jobs. With education, we can all earn more money, although for women we're still fighting for the basic human rights of wage parity. And with education we have better health, better hygiene, better nutrition, and better opportunities to build a solid foundation for our lives and those of our families.

Education isn't just about school books. It's not only about high school diplomas or college degrees or certifications that move us along our career path. Education means understanding. It means living and learning to respect one's self, to set boundaries, to understand our rights and speak up for them, to utilize ways in our society that help us elevate ourselves, our families and our world.

As an example, sexual assault continues to rise on college campuses. A recent study found that one out of four college women reported being been sexually abused while attending college, with one in eight reporting rape or attempted rape. This comes from a *Huffington Post* article, "Sexual Assault Will End Only If Students Start Learning About Healthy Relationships Starting in Kindergarten."

The article advocates for education of our children about healthy relationships, human and civil rights, sexual assault awareness in age appropriate presentations and discussions, and it strongly recommends a curriculum for college students with an interactive participation seminar on human sexuality and healthy relationships.

This is education, too—what my dad would call the school of hard knocks. The final test isn't on a piece of paper or a computerized form: it is in how we conduct our lives.

MY NEW HERO

Molly Melching, my new hero, whose story is told in the award-winning book *However Long the Night*, bears this out, too. Even as a child growing up in the Midwest, her life was directed by her heart. She knew her life would be different— over time and experiences in college and eventual philanthropic work, starting in 1974 when she landed in Senegal for a six-month study program that had been canceled, to her current achievements supporting human rights for women in the fight against female genital mutilation. She is a catalyst for change, utilizing education through her charitable organization, Tostan. The mission of Tostan is to empower African communities to bring about sustainable development and positive social transformation based on respect of human rights.

In particular, Molly and her organization gained international notice when they began their work partnering with communities to encourage abandonment of female genital cutting (FGC also referred to as FGM meaning female genital mutilation) and child/forced marriage.

Molly realized that not only was it taboo to speak about FGC among the communities, but the understanding of the harm it does to a woman's body and the rights of a woman to object to these procedures was not known. It was through education of the female body and education of human rights that the movement began first in one village and then spread to many.

As of April 2013, 5,423 communities in Senegal have publicly declared their abandonment of FGC after either participating in Tostan's program or through the process of "organized diffusion," spreading what they have learned among neighboring communities.

Molly started her inspiring work for change by understanding that education has many frames. People learn when they participate, and they create change when they have a voice in the outcome. She developed curricula and learning programs for communities in the villages that brought knowledge on many levels but primarily on women's rights and health, rights that had never been known or discussed. Just as important, she realized the power of decisions that were to be made as a group, not simply by one or two. It was through these group decisions based on knowledge, that the slow cog in a very big wheel started to turn toward condemnation of these practices by the people themselves.

At the end of the day, it was through learning about human dignity and explaining that all people—men, women and children—have inherent human rights, that the movement began. In this book about Molly Melching's journey, the author Aimee Molloy writes:

> "...up until these classes began through Tostan, women and girls had been taught that their role was to be obedient and submissive, at first to their fathers and then to their husbands. Beyond tending to their children and households, they hadn't any say in how their village or larger community was run. In fact, they had never been invited to village meetings where decisions were made; even if they had been, they would not have dared to speak."

Molly Melching is an inspiring educator and advocate for human rights. Yet it is through sharing knowledge and discussions that we learn what those rights are and can then decide for ourselves how to stand up for them.

GENDER EQUALITY FOR GIRLS THROUGH EDUCATION

It's the 21st century. Yes, we've made some progress and have created awareness of the need for girls to have equality and opportunity for education. But we're only scratching the surface. Girls' education is an intrinsic right and is critical to reaching development in many areas outside the classroom. Providing girls with an education helps break the cycle of poverty, both in developing countries and right here in the United States. Studies show that educated women are less likely to marry early and against their will…less likely to die in childbirth, more likely to have healthy babies, and more likely to send their children to school.

When education for girls is rooted in human rights and

gender equality, it effects the quality of life for generations to come. Strong organizations, such as UNICEF, Nike's Girl Effect and our own Women Like Us Foundation's One Girl at a Time program are turning to social education by tackling a developmental approach to not only academics but issues such as discrimination, violence, racism and girls' empowerment.

THE FACTS SPEAK FOR THEMSELVES

When a girl in the developing world receives seven years of education, she marries four years later and has 2.2 fewer children.

Secondary school completion rates for adolescent girls is below five percent in 19 sub-Saharan African countries.

In sub-Saharan Africa, fewer than one in five girls makes it to secondary school.

Girls who stay in school during adolescence have a later sexual debut, are less likely to be subjected to forced sex and, if sexually active are more likely to use contraception than their same-age peers who are out of school.

There are still 31 million girls of primary school age out of school. Of these, 17 million are expected never to enter school.

The Girl Effect Fact Sheet. www.girleffect.org

In the foreword of the 2009 report *Girls Count, A Global Investment and Action Agenda*, the authors make the case to the reader that if you want to change the world, invest in an adolescent girl.

They state that an adolescent girl stands at the threshold of adulthood. In that moment, much is decided. If she stays in school, remains healthy, and gains real skills, she will marry later, have fewer and healthier children, and earn an income that she'll invest back into her family.

But if she follows the path laid down by poverty, she'll leave school and enter marriage. As a girl mother, an unskilled worker, and an uneducated citizen, she'll miss out on the opportunity to reach her full human potential. And each individual tragedy, multiplied by millions of girls, will contribute to a much larger downward spiral for her nation.

MEETING IDA ODINGA

It was in the second week of our time in Kenya when the manager of the lodge where we were staying asked to speak with me. We had just returned from a long day being with the children at The N.A. Noël Preschool in Rusinga Island where we had helped them paint pictures about their lives with the art supplies we had carried with us from home.

"We have a visitor I would like to speak with you about, and I pray for your understanding," said James. He pointed toward the helicopter sitting on the front lawn. "Our former prime minister of Kenya, Raila Odinga, and his wife Ida Odinga, have landed here and would like to spend the night. As you know, our lodge is very small. Would you be willing to double up so that we can have a room open for them?"

I soon learned that Raila Odinga rewrote the constitution of Kenya during his time in office and is a strong voice for change and progress in Kenya. Little did I realize that myself and our small group of women and teen girls were about to meet an outstanding woman of kindness, compassion and a powerful advocate for education for women and girls and lauded as a champion for women's rights.

We were in the dining area, finishing our dinner and chatting about the day. Some of our team had gone to their rooms. Yet some wanted to linger. We wanted to understand who the Odingas are and were excited to be sharing our small lodge with them. Because we took up the dining room, James had set up a private table for them in his office. As the office door would swing open and shut from staff moving in and out, we could catch glimpses of the two of them.

Eventually the door of the office opened and the Odingas walked out. Ida Odinga walked past us. Sally, our producer and director of the documentary, took the risk. She asked Ida to join us for a glass of wine. Ida looked at our group and said, "Why not?"

And what a night that turned out to be. Ida talked with us about the status of women in Kenya—about the lack of education and equality for women. How women are marginalized in the majority of areas in Kenya. And how teen girls miss 5-6 days of school per month when they have their periods (due to lack of protection), eventually becoming so far behind in their classes that they drop out of school.

Her eyes lit up when she told us about establishing The Women's Voting League in 1991 that became known as the face of defiance during her country's one-party regime. She's been a champion of rights for women and girls in Kenya for more than two decades.

Our little dining room at the edge of Lake Victoria was the perfect setting for developing friendships and coming together in understanding of the work we can do to elevate women and girls here and at home. And then it got personal. She went on to tell us about the times she was teaching and raising her children on her own while her husband, Raila, was in prison for over eight years, yet was never tried or convicted and eventually became the Prime Minister of Kenya in 2008. She told us about the children she took into her home who had no place to go and who deserved a chance for a better life. She said, "I could always find a corner somewhere for one more of them." And she told us about times with her best friend, Winnie Mandela, who shared much of the same political abuse and strife with her husband Nelson Mandela as Ida did with Raila Odinga.

Sally and Catt then asked the question we had been wanting to ask for the last two hours. Would she be willing to let us film her in the morning for our documentary? We explained more about our project and how lucky we were to have an experienced filmmaker, award-winning journalist and accomplished videographer sitting at the table. Right then. Right there. We introduced our team. She said YES.

At 6 a.m. the following morning we met Ida on the lawn—videographer, director, interviewer all set to get on film the voice, words and wisdom of this woman.

When the interview was done, Raila Odinga walked out to the lawn and asked to meet us, be in a picture with us, and welcome us to his country.

Thank you, Ida, for writing the foreword for this book and speaking up for women and girls everywhere.

To Ida's point about girls and education, I became keenly aware that just bringing a few sanitary towels in our suitcases would make no real differences. Yes, we had a suitcase full to give to the teen girls in the villages on our trip. And when we came back we made sure to find donors to help us provide more. We were able to keep 55 girls in school during their periods for an entire year. It was a start, but I was determined it wouldn't be the end.

And it won't be. Because I met Celeste Mergens.

▼▼▼

▲▲▲

She knew there was something more she could do…she just couldn't put her finger on it. Celeste Mergens worked with girls in a Kenyan orphanage and knew it was important for them to have textbooks, water and food. But there was something else. In the middle of the night it came to her. All the textbooks in the world couldn't keep girls in school if they missed 5-6 days a month while on their menstrual cycle.

Celeste founded a grassroots network of sewing volunteers, designed sustainable feminine hygiene kits and now helps keep girls in school for 2-3 years with one kit. Girls no longer need to sit in grass or on dirt during their periods. They now have a better chance for an education.

▼▼▼

Celeste Mergens

I AM MORE THAN WHERE I LIVE

❝ SOMETIMES CIRCUMSTANCE 'TEACHES' US TO IDENTIFY WITH IT, IF WE CHOOSE TO LET IT. DON'T LET IT. ❞

I was five years old and our family was living out of a car at a roadside stop when I realized that people don't know who you are just by looking at you or your circumstances. You have to know that for yourself.

My stepfather was always searching for "greener pastures"—a better job and a better life in yet another, then another, then another, place. We moved from state to state 32 times before I was 13. The lullaby of the road helped me forget the crowding of the back seat where my three sisters and I tagged along with my stepdad and my mother. Roadside rest stops and state parks served as our temporary homes. I didn't mind the parks. They were always interesting, and I loved being with my sisters. However, I didn't love the stale, day-old tuna fish sandwiches, crunchy on the outside, mushy in the middle, that would "do us" for days to stave off hunger.

One day at the state park where we temporarily resided, I was admiring the sparkling sidewalks and feeling the warmth of the sun on my bare feet. A woman approached, walking her dog. I was captivated by its rhinestone collar until she threw away a perfectly good, half-eaten apple. I followed its arch and thump into the bottom of the garbage bin, trying to decide whether to climb into the bin after it. As I was puzzling over what to do, I noticed the woman was looking me up and down, her nose crinkled up—as if I had just offered her one of my day-old tuna fish sandwiches.

"Where are your shoes, girl?" she asked.

I stood as tall as I could. "I'm toughing my feet," I said. She didn't need to know we were in-between schools. Or that I had the habit of standing so my shoes wore out on the sides. Or that even though my mom shaved down the heels to level them, she could no longer rescue them. Shoes? I had no shoes. Shoes would have to wait.

I sensed what she saw when she looked at me, at my bare feet, my too-small clothes. For just a moment, I saw myself the way she saw me, and I felt small and poor and pitiful. Then a sudden warm assurance came over me that I was not what she saw. I wanted to tell her as much: "I am not from here. I am not what you see!" But before I could answer, she was gone.

In that moment and many moments since, I have felt that wave of unexpected assurance that I am more than where I live. I am not my clothes. I am not my hunger. I am not my economic circumstances. I am not my physical appearance. I knew then—and I know even better today—that each one of us is far greater than we can possibly comprehend, and each one of us has something to contribute.

I KNEW WHAT IT FELT LIKE TO GO HUNGRY

Later, in 2008, I was in Kenya, Africa, seeking solutions to help reverse cycles of poverty. I had a passion to lift communities by helping them change their circumstances and was working with the Clay Foundation and their initiative in support of Project Education, Inc., headquartered in a very arid and remote area, called Ngomano. My work centered on creating sustainable solutions for global communities with few resources. I also volunteered with an orphanage and school in Dagoretti whenever I was in Kenya.

After widespread post-election violence, I found myself working harder to help the orphanage weather the after-effects. By October 2008, the orphanage had gone from a far-too-crowded 420 children under their care to housing a reported 1,400 children packed into a scant, rudimentary, corrugated-iron facility.

Though I had returned to the States, I was doing everything I could to help feed the children, but I finally reached the point where my resources and connections were tapped out. Then came the night I received the telephone call: "We are completely out of food and have been for several days." I knew what it felt like to go hungry. I wanted desperately to help but there was nothing more that I could do.

As a woman of faith, I did the only thing I could do. I knelt and pled for any ideas or ways to get food to those needy children. Nothing came to me. NOTHING. I fell asleep while still pleading.

Suddenly, I woke at 2:30 a.m. with the thought running through my head: "Have you asked what the girls are doing for feminine hygiene?" I gasped. I had considered many things communities were dealing with due to scarcity of sustainable natural resources, and lack of access to education. But I had never even thought to ask once what the girls were doing for feminine hygiene.

I ran to the computer and sent an email posing the question. The answer I received was stunning: "Nothing. They sit in their rooms." How was that possible? Two or three girls shared each of the beds. The center informed me that the girls waited on a piece of cardboard. I was struck by the enormity of the problems of such conditions: girls would miss several days of school every month, fall behind, miss opportunities—all because of a natural biological function and an unmet need. In that orphanage alone there were 500 girls, sitting alone in their rooms every month for days.

Throughout those night and early morning hours I considered what I should do. If I sent money for disposable pads and the center needed food, they would use the money for food. Anyone would.

WHAT WAS NEEDED WAS SOMETHING SUSTAINABLE

With what little information I had, I went to work to address the problem of feminine hygiene, initially solely for the 500 girls at the center. I was to leave for Kenya again in three-and-a-half weeks. In just a few days, two design solutions, chosen from many options, became our first prototypes. Miraculously, in that short time, wonderful volunteers dove in to make the first 500 Days for Girls kits.

Now we just had to help the girls with the need until we traveled there. Reaching out, I found a lone nonprofit providing disposable feminine hygiene products at wholesale cost. I secured funding for food and disposable products to last until we arrived with a washable pad solution, and both were delivered to the orphanage in Dagoretti. We soon discovered that there was another problem with the pads besides affordability: disposable is not disposable in many global communities that are without even the most rudimentary sanitation systems. Disposables, undisposed of, only resulted in additional health issues. They clogged the latrines, were tucked into chinks of the chain-link fence adjacent to the latrines, piled against posts or on the ground. Some girls even tried to wash and reuse them.

When we arrived with those first washable Days for Girls kits meant to mitigate a specific problem, I was stunned to learn the broader implications for girls and women who lack menstrual supplies. I found out that girls not only sat in their rooms during menses on a piece of cardboard for days at a time, but many had been sexually exploited in exchange for disposable pads. This is one of many of the hideous prices some girls pay throughout the world to gain access to feminine hygiene products. There was even more that these women and girls had to teach us.

Our first designs were terrible, often ineffective or unworkable in places where menses is taboo. Yet while we made many mistakes, we listened, and we responded quickly to the physical and cultural needs of the women. Today, after testing and utilizing 28 different patterns, Days for Girls washable feminine hygiene kits are comfortable, adjust to the personal flow of the user, and can be washed using very little water. They don't look like pads and they dry quickly, all things that the women and girls told us were important. Further, the kits are proving to last an average of two to three years.

Days for Girls kits are the genius of many women who worked together across cultures, languages, and ethnicities. The cultural, physical, and environmental relevance of Days for Girls kits are a testament to what listening and collaboration can do. Days for Girls kits are the result of the collaborative efforts of individuals who recognize no one person can understand the entirety of a problem, yet each person can bring a unique talent, vision, and perspective to the problem that will synergize into a collective wisdom.

Strangely, growing up in poverty and being homeless has been a gift to me. I know what poverty is. I know what it feels like. Because of my experiences, there is no judgment of persons or places, only complete confidence that we can create positive solutions together.

CIRCUMSTANCES CAN AND DO CHANGE

They change when many perspectives are brought to bear on the challenges we face in today's world. They especially change when those who have the resources to effect solutions to problems honor the wisdom of those they seek to aid and assist.

What have I learned over many years of searching for solutions aimed at reversing poverty? What will empower the communities and individuals who experience poverty? I have learned what I never would have guessed—that providing menstrual supplies is a key to greater access to education, health, confidence, and well-being for women. I have learned that a lack of access to quality supplies is a global issue, even in Western nations, including the U.S. The need for education and menstrual supplies has been hidden in stigma and shame, until now.

Since 2008, Days for Girls has reached and provided supplies to more than 300,000 women and girls in more than 100 nations on six continents. Millions of women around the globe have faced the consequences of not having what they need for their monthly cycle, all because we didn't ask. What other questions are we not asking? When we ask the right questions and identify the need, those with resources should provide help.

However, we can only truly help once we recognize and affirm the wisdom of the very people we are working with in knowing what solutions work for them. Their resourcefulness and their ability is often far greater than any wisdom we might impart and anything we might give them. Only by trusting their wisdom, and recognizing the beauty in their cultures and traditions can workable solutions be developed. Building what will work in countries that experience poverty and that lack resources must involve learning from and teaching one another. It must be done without shaming and without a feeling of superiority, because true relief is about finding keys to empower individuals in communities in need so they can identify and implement their own solutions.

For example, in the 2015 earthquake in Nepal, over 9,000 people died and more than 24,000 were injured. Hundreds of thousands of people were made homeless and in some areas entire villages were leveled. Women were prey to greater levels of sexual violence and trafficking. Right after the earthquake,

Mercy Corps came out with a report that five things were needed: tarps, clean water, blankets and towels, cooking utensils, and washable feminine hygiene. Why did feminine hygiene come up? Because of an illegal but still practiced tradition called *chaupadi*, where women and girls must dwell in sheds during menstruation and are not permitted in the home or even on the pathway to the home. After the earthquake, when so many were in tents, there was no away to send the women to. Suddenly there was no enforcing the tradition and the need was clear. A tradition can only change when conversations about menstruation change from within. A shift happens when people are invited to consider, rather than being told what to do.

Based on these collaborative principles and concepts, a phenomenal global network of 720+ Days for Girls chapters and teams of volunteers in 17 nations have made tens of thousands of Days for Girls kits. Days for Girls Ambassadors of Women's Health go to countries in need and distribute kits and provide education.

Days for Girls regional centers have also been established in a number of countries. These grassroots, women-led social enterprises create long-term and sustainable access to menstrual hygiene management education and materials, within their own communities.

Days for Girls micro-enterprises are now empowering local communities by creating jobs, providing resources for micro-businesses to make and sell Days for Girls kits, and supporting community-led initiatives dedicated to improving access to women's health education and advocacy. This unique hybrid approach will ensure that women not only have affordable, sustainable, quality hygiene continuously, but given proper education, they will break down the shame and stigma associated with menstruation in many of these communities while creating jobs and increasing safety for women, girls, families and communities.

Days for Girls is helping to ensure that girls and women can go to school and go to work, and do so with greater health, opportunity and dignity. Who would have guessed that supplying feminine hygiene kits was key to reversing cycles of poverty and violence against women?

I would never have guessed. But I listened.

I still dislike tuna fish sandwiches. And I still am not from *here*. Everywhere I travel throughout the world, I am at home, and I am filled with admiration for a world of amazing people, coming from different countries, cultures, ethnicities and languages—individuals of great wisdom and strength who are far more than their circumstances.

In a very real way, I am not the founder of Days for Girls. Days for Girls was inspired, and the volunteers and champions along the way hold creation and possession of it with me. I am, however, the really good listener who pays attention, shows up and keeps working. I will keep doing so until we have reached Every Girl. Everywhere. Period.

Celeste Mergens-Founder Days for Girls

▲▲▲

Women locally and globally are standing up for education. Wendy Kopp is one of them. What a brilliant step forward for college students and teens around the nation through her program, Teach for America.

Teach for America began in 1989 when Wendy Kopp wrote her senior thesis at Princeton University. The nonprofit started over 25 years ago and has become one of the most progressive, powerful and meaningful movements for underserved children in our schools.

Wendy proposed a theory that if we could recruit high-performing college grads to teach in high-need urban and rural schools, and more leaders would make education their life's work while understanding the issues for underserved children at the classroom level, change can happen.

By recruiting college seniors and offering an opportunity to partner with schools and mentor and teach their challenged students for a two-year commitment, her program could develop more teachers and improve the opportunities for children's futures.

The statistics are staggering. There are 16 million children growing up in poverty in the United States. When children grow up in poverty, by the third grade they are typically one-and-a-half years behind in school. And by 8th grade, they are three years behind. They are half as likely to graduate high school and one-tenth as likely to graduate from college as students from affluent environments.

Wendy has created a movement fighting for educational equity. Everyone has a right to learn. The Teach for America website points out that children's education in our country depends on where they live, what their parents earn, and the color of their skin. Her movement to right this social injustice brings diverse and passionate people who start in low-income classrooms with their partner school.

Wendy's mantra: One day all children in this nation will have the opportunity to attain an excellent education.

Now, 26 years later, what started as an idea for a thesis has grown to a community of 50,000+ teachers, and has reached over 10 million children.

▲▲▲

Deb Myers has worked diligently in developing a mentoring program for teen girls. It's called One Girl at a Time and is supported by the Women Like Us foundation. She understands the importance of resources and on-the-ground education and experiences that can get a girl a chance for a better future. Through self-esteem building, boundary setting and lively yet important discussions on sex trafficking, homelessness, gender bias and more, these girls have an opportunity for a stronger and bolder voice for their future. You can hear the change in the girls' stories.

▼▼▼

Deb Myers
PREYING ON INNOCENCE

> ❝ KNOWING THAT TEEN PREGNANCY AND SUICIDE HAVE SKYROCKETED **PROPELS ME FORWARD TO FIGHT** FOR THEM…ONE GIRL AT A TIME. ❞

I have often been called an advocate for teen girls. I love that label; however, I am truly an advocate for ALL women. I believe a woman's strength, compassion and ability to find the best in people enables females to empower one another. For so long now, we have been, in a sense, brainwashed. We have allowed the media and workplace to determine our personal sense of self-worth. We have been programmed to believe that pink is our color of choice. We have been told that we can become nurses but not doctors.

We have digested the misconception that we must all aesthetically emulate supermodels to be seen as beautiful. Though I believe our society has sought to make strides for the benefit of the female, in many ways we have not. I come from a generation where leading career opportunities were left for men, despite the fact that a household required two incomes to forge ahead. There's a silent understanding that the mother will take care of the family, support her husband as head of the household, and be successful in her career, as well. For generations, we have battled this expectation of the modern female, while also facing societal struggles of idealistic stereotyping.

MY MOTHER'S LESSON

So many women today never take the time to explore who they are, until their children are grown and there is more time for self-reflection. As women, we often put our own needs and self-development last. When our children are grown and there's a moment of silence, many of us don't know what we want or who we are outside of our family dynamics. Often we lose hope and never live a fulfilled and truly balanced life.

We have attempted this tightrope balancing act for generations. My own mother, who came from a culture far more prehistoric than ours, entered the United States at the age of 15. She has said that is when her life truly began. She desired to leave her family in the pursuit of becoming an American woman, with freedom and opportunity. Soon after, she embraced the ability to have a voice, to make her own future, and to have value. This is the voice she raised within me. Looking back now, it is certainly why I have had a very strong sense of self. It is my mother's lesson, my mother's voice within me.

I remember the day I decided to dedicate my life to advocating for teen girls. I had been invited to the home of a woman creating awareness on human sex trafficking. As she described the mentality behind how the predators seek out potential victims, my stomach turned. She explained to me that girls were selected between the ages of 12 and 18, when they are the most vulnerable. She explained that most victims were innocent girls from wonderful families; the predators are preying on innocence. It is our vulnerable youth who are targeted. Predators understand the concepts of acquiring their victims with youth, with purity, at a time when they are in great need of direction, affection, and love. These young women care so much about issues like: "Why am I not a size one? Why don't I have a boyfriend?"

Teens are preyed upon physically and mentally because of lack of confidence and then they are brainwashed. In sex trafficking, a young woman is told she is beautiful, she is told that she will have money, and oftentimes she is courted by a handsome young man, a new boyfriend, all under false pretenses. In the end she fears she will be killed and is left with no self-worth. To her, her life is over. So many survivors of trafficking, runaways, homeless and victims of addiction, will tell you that they got in their position because they were looking for a void to be filled, for happiness and love. Many can't explain why they stayed in that situation.

Reflecting now on many cultures all over the world, preying on innocence is at the heart of inequality, denied education, inhibited self-worth and the lack of progression of women as equals. Break a woman down so she is weak: she can't fight, she loses hope and she is powerless to achieve the advancement of herself or others. Beat down her pride and value as a human, and she is silenced. Treat her as if she is less important, and she is subdued. Uplift her, educate her, love her and empower her, and she will fight for herself and for others.

Why, after generations, are we still not further along? Women are still objectified, are underpaid, and continue to strive for gender equality. What, as a society, are we teaching young women? Counselors in schools can't counsel like they used to because of liability issues and lack of time (oftentimes there are 250 students per counselor). Television does not portray equality. Women in leadership positions are insignificant in percentages.

I decided I would create awareness of my own. I would live my life for a purpose. I would incorporate empowerment to young women into my personal journey. I would direct the life my path would take. I would reach in at this vulnerable place in life and teach girls about their value as women, create awareness on topics like sex trafficking, bullying, and healthy coping skills. I would create a sisterhood that generates open discussion, support of each other and confidence. I would tackle struggles they face today, open their eyes and redirect the path of what may have been bad choices to be those that would change the world. Together we would shout from the rooftops, "I am beautiful!" But, I understood this would not be an easy road. Statistics say one in every four girls doesn't have anyone she can turn to for help.

EVEN ONE GIRL MAKES A DIFFERENCE

I started the One Girl at a Time Program because I knew one thing for sure: If I started with one, that would create impact, and that would help her to be strong and raise her children to be wise and empowered. And if that grew to thousands, how wonderful would that be? I have seen young women who once bowed their head in shame and guilt soon hold their chin high, because they realized they had a gift. They had experiences they could share, love to give and arms to hold those who needed them. We all need this—we just need to learn the power it has to create change.

So many of our young women in One Girl at a Time have said, "I am only me." But by focusing on them as amazing already, by offering them the tools to make good decisions, their confidence flourishes. These confident young women lead. They fight for justice. They dream bigger and they believe they can have impact to better the world. Why? Because we, as role models who simply can, care enough about them to uplift them, to share what we know and pass it along. Girls have said to me, "I never knew so many girls were stressed out like me and had the pressures I do; so many have problems at home or have faced the hardships I have. I understand I am not alone. I don't want this program to be over."

I say to them, "Oh, honey, it's not over: it's just beginning."

Teach our young women their strengths and they will take flight. Enable them to be brave and bold and it will cause a ripple effect on the world in all areas of need. We have to fight for our youth. Sex trafficking in the United States is just below drug sales as the most profitable criminal activity. Knowing that teen pregnancy and suicide have skyrocketed propels me forward to fight for them...One Girl at a Time!

Within hours of meeting with teen girls and showing we care, they beam with excitement, because the burden is lifted from their shoulders to try to aspire to become something they believed to be unattainable. Remove the objectification and treat them as equals, and half the battle is gone. Standards set by society and stereotyping are what restrict them, and soon they understand they must create a future with self-esteem and drive to get ahead. That is my passion: teaching these young women their value, beautiful as they are. I want to lift them up so they can see their futures, love themselves, and see who they can become.

LET'S TEACH LIVING LIFE ON PURPOSE

Let's teach women and girls to live their life on purpose. We should unite and embrace who we are. Together we can pursue our dreams and lift each other up, emotionally, physically, and spiritually. Together, let's raise our daughters to believe they can be anything they want, and, most importantly, teach them to love each other—teach them to fight stereotypes and forge forward. Let's support those fighting the important fights, so horrific acts like female genital mutilation, rape and human sex trafficking cease to exist, because we have pushed hard for human equality. Let's embrace women of all shapes, colors and sizes. Let's break down the walls that hold us back. Let's take hold of the arms of those who have lost hope and tell them we care. Let's push for our laws, policies and rules to promote equality, punish perpetrators and protect the innocent.

There is a movement on the rise. Can you feel it? Women in

Hollywood, in the workplace and in the home have had enough. They are forging forward with their chins held high. They know the struggle and it has been going on far too long. I want to be an agent for change. I am not a Congresswoman; I'm not a CEO of a corporation; I'm not anyone famous. I am me! I am a mom, a wife and an interior designer. But first, I am a woman. I am passionate and strong. I am, like all of us, here for a reason. This is my calling, lifting each other up to see beyond the fence and saying, "You are amazing and beautiful. See, this is where your life can go—your dreams are right there. All you have to do is just reach out and take them, and you can do it!"

Deb Myers-One Girl at A Time Program

▲▲▲
One of the girls who could have benefitted from Deb's One Girl at a Time Program (had there been one in her school years ago), was Elissa Kravetz. When in middle school, Elissa was bullied. Her story here will sadden your heart. Yet, the eventual strength and resilience she found is testimony to the importance of self-acceptance and love of ourselves. A good lesson for all of us, and particularly important to teens.
▼▼▼

Elissa Kravetz

RADICAL SELF-ACCEPTANCE. KINDNESS. THIS IS HOW THE WORLD WILL CHANGE AND EVOLVE FOR THE BETTER.

> ❝ ONE GIRL SOLD TICKETS FOR $1 SO KIDS COULD WATCH ME GET BEAT UP AFTER SCHOOL. ❞

My name is Elissa Kravetz and I am a woman. A goddess. A mother. A sister. A daughter. A friend. A woman who at times is fearless. Afraid. Bold. Excited. Happy. Sad. Adventurous. Introverted. Extroverted. I'm made up of many intricacies, feelings and thoughts. Most of all, I'm made up of LOVE. I have so much love to give, share, and express. It wasn't until 2010 as I embarked on my own personal and spiritual journey when I realized how powerful I am. How powerful WE ALL ARE. I firmly believe we can all do something that can inspire, help and contribute in the world.

I started working in public relations immediately upon

graduating from college. I was introduced to Steve Madden while still in school and I talked my way into an internship with him. This internship turned into an in-house public relations position with the Steve Madden Company. After working for Steve in-house for three years, I moved to Los Angeles, California to open my very own public relations firm.

Approximately 11 years after graduation, I was running the Los Angeles office of my agency, partnered with my sister. We had wonderful offices, dedicated employees, and a strong client base. Despite all appearances that I was running a successful business, I knew something was missing. I wasn't personally fulfilled; I knew there was more. On a leap of faith, I decided to step out of my box, out from my comfort zone, and venture on my own to embark on my personal "Eat, Pray, Love" journey. I began studying at the Kabbalah Centre. I traveled to Bali, India and Thailand. I spent many hours in meditation, exploring my spirituality through the practice of yoga. It was then that I realized how much the hardships of my childhood and youth, the effects of being bullied in my younger years, had impacted my life and personal sense of self.

I had never before discussed the adversities I faced in my youth, but once I started exploring this private and personal pain of my past, I couldn't stop. I was asked to speak at schools and camps. I was asked to become a spokesperson and advocate for youth, to speak to those young girls and boys who are enduring similar circumstances, who are currently exposed to unnecessary victimization.

WHY DID THIS HAPPEN TO ME?

I remember it like it was yesterday. I was 12 years old, in seventh grade, and received the dreadful phone call from a friend who said, "Lauren is mad at you!" Lauren was my best friend at the time. My BFF. We were close for years, even dressed up as BFFs for Halloween. I came into school one day and she didn't want to be my friend anymore. Lauren mad at me, turned into three friends mad at me – five friends, 10 – eventually our entire "group" stopped talking to me. My boyfriend broke up with me. We had a large grade school and middle school, so when I would go outside of our group to make new friends, rumors were spread. Eventually the entire grade and entire school was against me. I had DIE BITCH spray-painted in black letters on my locker. I had gum and eggs thrown at me in the cafeteria. After eating for weeks in the nurse's office and pretending to be sick, I started spending lunch in the bathroom, sitting on the toilet in a stall with my legs up so nobody would know I was in there.

I received a letter with 300 signatures: at the top it read, "Below is a list of people who promise to make your life a living hell. You should either move or KILL YOURSELF." One girl sold tickets for $1 so kids could watch me get beat up after school. This abusive treatment went on for months. I slept in bed with my parents each night, having so much anxiety about going to school. Yet each morning I wasn't going let them get the best of me, so again I would go to school and endure the treatment and ridicule. My parents went to the school and visited the houses of the other kids, but nothing worked. "Why did this happen to me?" is the question I am most often asked when I lead a school assembly. "What did I do wrong?" And, the answer is…nothing. I did absolutely nothing to deserve this vicious treatment. No one deserves this! Why are people cruel? People are cruel because they don't feel good. Happy people are kind. People who are filled with confidence and joy behave outwardly with LOVE.

RADICAL SELF-ACCEPTANCE

Before I knew it, I took a $400 check that was given to me from an overnight camp and I opened a bank account, starting a nonprofit organization called The Farley Project. When I speak at schools with The Farley Project, I share how bullies are not bad people, they simply don't feel good. They need a hug.

Need to be heard. To be seen. This goes on into our adult lives, when we are tired or not feeling our best. This is when we yell at our parents, children, husbands. It's a cycle. The answer is self-love. Self-care. In our society we are taught at a young age to put such a high price on success, working long hours, and making money, and less emphasis on self-love, kindness, sharing, giving, volunteering. We must practice doing the things that fill ourselves up so we can overflow and give and share and love others. The one thing that kids who are being bullied need to hear over and over and over again is that it's NOT THEM. There is nothing wrong with them. They are beautiful and magical and special and worthy of all of the love in the world. Everyone is! Radical self-acceptance. Kindness. This is how the world will change and evolve for the better.

I recently had my 39th birthday. This happened to me 27 years ago and there are still certain songs that remind me of seventh grade. When I hear them I cry—a cry that comes from somewhere deep within me. This has shaped my life in so many ways…some beautiful, some I wish to let go of. I still feel fear at times that friends will stop liking me. I still have fear that I've done something wrong when I don't hear back from someone. It is an imprint that runs so deep within my heart. My big compassionate overflowing heart, a heart that has so much love to give.

THE FARLEY PROJECT

With The Farley Project we have two programs. We have all-grade and all-school assemblies. This is when myself and one of our ambassadors goes into the school and we openly share about our real, raw experiences with what we've been through. Every assembly we've done has resonated so well with the students, we always leave at least 30 minutes for a question-and-answer forum, as our stories allow the students a safe space to share. And often when kids are being bullied, they are so embarrassed and ashamed that they don't talk about it. We always stay after for impromptu break-out sessions with the kids, as well, as several of them like to speak with us in private. In addition to our assemblies we have a 10-week love and kindness curriculum. This is when we come into the school each week for an hour and work with a small group of students. We usually take over a teacher's class or our program is implemented into the health curriculum. We bring journals for the students and each week has a theme. We sit in a circle and start with a breathing meditation to have the kids present. Everyone shares. We have beautiful exercises and it's extremely therapeutic. In one school there was a student who has been tormented for years and none of the kids in the group knew this was going on. They all made a pact to love and protect him from that day forward. We had 15-year-olds hugging and crying; it was beautiful! We bring in hand mirrors and have the kids look into their own eyes and recite positive affirmations. The program is truly powerful.

We worked with an inner-city school a few years ago in Inglewood, CA. We spent 10 weeks with a group of seventh grade kids. This was a rough school. Many of their parents were in jail; a lot of the kids were on welfare and were scared to walk home from school because of the tough neighborhood. The kids found peace in the hour they spent with us. Each week they would ask for the meditation. They were so excited to share with us how they completed their homework each week. When we came back the following year for a follow-up, we were brought out to the gym to overlook the entire eighth grade class. The students who had taken part in our curriculum were literally standing taller. Brighter. They had a confidence and light that was not to be missed. We listened to them. We saw them. We were kind to them and taught them how to share kindness with others. It was miraculous what took place at that school!

In addition to The Farley Project, I'm currently in the process of creating a brand with a family in South India called Sun

Child. I met the family on a trip to Goa last year and have been curating a line of their one-of-a-kind silk dresses to sell here in the United States. I'm donating a portion of the sales to an orphanage in Rishikesh called Ramana's Garden.

NOT JUST ABOUT BULLYING

My advocacy does not only consist of my efforts to bring awareness to anti-bullying. I hope to support and inspire people in all facets of life. I want to share my experience and what I have learned about the importance of human-to-human contact and love. We *all* have the power to make a difference. We all have 24 hours in a day; it's about how we use them. Looking people in the eye when you talk with them, really listening to what the people around you have to say. Giving a hug, a real hug, lending an ear, a shoulder, or even money, anything that can help someone else have a good day—that's what I'm passionate about.

Oh, the juicy challenges along the way! *Life* is a challenge. Balancing my desire to give to the world, to others and to myself is a challenge. Shutting down my brain to relax is a challenge. Feeling like I'm not doing enough is a challenge. Getting up and delivering an assembly to 1,100 students is a challenge. Traveling back and forth 30 hours to India twice in one summer to get a brand started was a challenge. Yet when I look at all of these challenges, I also see so many incredible blessings. Major blessings! The fact that I get to inspire others is a blessing. The fact that I know enough and have made self-care and self-love a priority is a blessing. The fact that I was able to work with my sister is a blessing. Sharing in front of an auditorium of students (although I get unbelievably nervous) is a blessing. And traveling back and forth to India…well, India has a very special place in my heart. And, to be able to go there for work is a huge blessing.

Everything in life is about polarities; everything has two sides, light and dark, up and down, love and fear. When I'm feeling anxious over the challenges (which is often), I breathe, take a yoga class, walk to the ocean with my dog or cook. I try to relax my mind, be open and allow myself the opportunity to feel my feelings, and then let them pass. I also have a wonderful support system of friends and family whom I lean on often. I try to show up and be as loving, present, kind and authentic as I can every day. Some days I'm better at it than others. But this is always my intention.

We all have the power to make a difference. Be honest with yourself. Be honest with how you want to spend your time and with what brings you joy and happiness. Tune in to your heart as much as possible. We all have the voice of the heart and the head and I am a big believer in listening to the heart. This is where your intuition comes from. Be fearless in the pursuit of what makes you happy. If you want to travel, travel! If you want to paint, paint! If you want to dance, dance! In almost all of my endeavors there were naysayers who were cautioning me because of their own fear. Listen to your inner voice first and let that guide you. Be your own biggest cheerleader. Write affirmations in lipstick on your mirror. Love yourself and love yourself well. And, go out and be a warrior in this world!

Elissa Kravetz-Founder of The Farley Project and Sun Child

▲▲▲

Laura Henderson is an educator, too. She's not in the classroom. She's not on the streets. She's in her garden. A garden which eventually was the catalyst for a thriving nonprofit, Growing Places. I love that name. Because while she's teaching and collaborating on the importance of good nutrition, her work goes beyond the physical, and transcends to the soul. Laura has committed her life to empower others by educating and opening opportunities for good health and wholeness for others. And she credits her mentors and teachers along the way for opening her eyes to opportunities that she can now share with others.

▼▼▼

Laura Henderson

GROW WELL, EAT WELL, LIVE WELL, BE WELL

> **❝ I BEGAN TO SEE ALL THE WAYS GARDENS, AND THE ACT OF GARDENING, PROVIDED PERFECT METAPHORS FOR LIFE.... ❞**

WELLNESS

It is my belief that every human shares the same essential desire to be well: to be vibrant, healthy, thriving. At the same time, we do not all have the resources, privilege, life circumstances and experiences that can be great ingredients for the path to being well. And, even when we do, we still don't necessarily find the path.

At our essence we are all whole, not broken. I am tremendously grateful to have had mentors, guides and teachers who have empowered me forward on the path to realizing my capacity and wellness. While it isn't a space I live in all the time, I have been there enough now to know it is real and achievable. I also have come to understand that being well isn't an experience or state someone else gives you or keeps from you. As one of my teachers says, no one can do the work for you, and you can't do it alone. That's why I've committed my life and work to being present, to shepherd and empower others on their own path to vibrancy, health and thriving—just as I continue to do the same work within my own life and my own path.

WHERE MY INNER WORK BEGAN

In 2007, I attended an event at CITYOGA in Indianapolis, with an internationally renowned yoga teacher, Seane Corn. It was a detox workshop. I had signed up for this particular workshop because I had been feeling for several years like there was some toxic element in my body that I was working to purge; I knew I had some inner trauma to work through.

There was one area in particular that was close to my heart: the unexpected death of my only brother who had died in a car accident in 2004 at the age of 18. As it turned out, Seane's words transformed my life far more than any physical yoga practice ever had or could. Her words and the conversation she fostered between attendees sparked a new understanding within me of the inextricable interconnectedness of body, mind and spirit.

Seane guided me into a deeper understanding, and made real the concept of emotional toxicity and the physical body. Her guidance and words set me on a path of exploring this interconnectedness in my life, and how toxicity was holding me back from fulfilling my capacity to be well. I heard truth spoken and it called up the voice of my own soul. I began working through these toxic elements; I began embracing life as someone who manifests, who loves, as someone who leads and thrives, rather than identifying as a victim of circumstances, waiting for someone else to take the lead, for someone else to make things better, for someone else to ease my grief and to "save me" in some way.

LEARNING THE CONNECTION BETWEEN THE BODY AND SOUL

Around the same time, I met a farmer named Debbie

Apple. Debbie raised dairy cows on 100 percent grass for the production of unpasteurized milk. I traded Debbie a weekly private yoga class in my home for a gallon of raw milk. After her class, we would spend another hour or so talking about how she got into farming, why she and her then-husband transitioned from conventional grain-based dairy to 100 percent grass-fed, the difference in how the human body processes and converts these two types of dairy, the relationship between cancer and food products coming out of the relatively new "industrial" agriculture model, the emerging concerns about genetically engineered foods, the challenges of being a small or mid-size farm, and much more.

When I listened to Debbie I felt as if the cells in my body and brain would light up and vibrate, like they were screaming, "This is truth! Listen!" I also felt angry at what was being done to us by the food industry. When I met Seane I was reminded I didn't have to be a victim. I could do something. Though nothing could bring back my brother, finding purpose in other ways began to ease the pain of that loss. I went home and told my husband, we either needed to do something to make Indianapolis a place we wanted to live, or we needed to move. But move where? No place is perfect—until you see the wholeness in it.

I started doing more yoga and leadership trainings with Seane Corn and the organization she started with Hala Khouri and Suzanne Sterling, called Off the Mat, Into the World. I learned I didn't have to be able to solve all the world's problems, or even to solve all the food system problems, to make a difference. I also learned that I had to start by creating the change I wanted to see in my own life and my own community, as Ghandi said.

MAKING THE CHANGE TO WELLNESS IN MY LIFE

I started "doing something" by changing my relationship to food and the sources of my food. I learned to garden, bought directly from farmers, visited their farms and learned about their farming practices. I began eating whole foods and preparing meals at home from scratch. I've been vegetarian by choice since a very young age, and never ate a lot of fast food, but I started cutting out processed foods all together. As I did, I began to notice how much better I felt when I ate whole, vibrant, living foods, and how truly toxic I felt when I ate processed food, or even certain things like soy, corn, sugar, too much cheese or ice cream, or a lot of bread. My body began to feel more awake, resilient, and strong. My mental state was more positive, proactive, and creative. And I wanted to share my transformation with others. I wanted more people to have this experience!

GROWING PLACES INDY WAS BORN

In 2008, I started the Indy Winter Farmers Market as a way of supporting the farmers who were making it possible for me to eat well, and to make it easier for others in my community to eat well, too. In 2009, the opportunity was presented to start a garden and urban farming summer internship at White River State Park (WRSP) in downtown Indianapolis, visited by more than three million people each year. I developed the initial vision for one garden with a friend, and presented it at Pecha Kucha Vol. 7: The Next Indianapolis. The event was part of the Spirit and Place Festival, and the winning idea was to be awarded $10,000 toward the project. I won for my presentation "Growing Place: The Slow Food Edible Garden at White River State Park." And, Growing Places Indy was born.

By 2011, I felt I needed to be connecting the "grow well" component of the urban farming internship and demonstration garden, and the "eat well" component of the Indy Winter Farmers Market, and produce now being grown at WRSP, with the yoga component that had been and remained such a vital element in my personal experience. I tried offering some mindful eating workshops at yoga studios where I was teaching already, but what I really wanted to do was bring yoga—physically and philosophically—into the work of Growing Places Indy.

I began by introducing yoga and mindfulness concepts in the summer internship program, and the response was incredible. People started making the same kinds of life-changing, profoundly empowering self-realizations that I had made. I wasn't telling them what to think or do; I was simply opening a space of exploration that most had not entered before. I began to see all the ways gardens, and the act of gardening, provided perfect metaphors for life…such as identifying and weeding out our limiting beliefs. And thus the "live well" component of yoga, mindfulness practices, and personal inquiry took root in our education programs, complementing experience-based gardening, cooking and nutrition education so body, mind and spirit all find nourishment.

LIFE OPENS WITH AN ABUNDANCE

It has been an amazing journey thus far, and I am truly excited to see where the future leads. I have discovered that when you align to what resonates as truth in ways that are affirming, loving, empowering and uplifting, life opens with an abundance of possibility, support and opportunity. People who share a common vision show up at just the right moment to offer support while following their own dreams in a way that strengthens the whole. That isn't to say there aren't falls, flops, failures, loss and moments of heartbreak. Of course there are. The difference is I'm learning to accept the opportunity to learn and love more from those experiences, to spend less time in the fear and despair zone when they occur, and to trust in both my own resiliency and the natural phenomenon of expansion and contraction.

There is nothing—be it idea, program, organization, person, plant, structure, cultural phenomenon or otherwise—that doesn't go through the full cycle of life from birth to death, to the recycling of energy, matter, material, concept or otherwise that brings forward the next iteration of the cycle. Part of the path to being well is remembering and trusting this cycle.

It seems it is not in our innate human nature to do so, and thus it requires practice. I catch myself when my mind starts to spiral away from visions of wholeness into fears of everything falling apart. I take some deep breaths and choose to reset my thinking along with my behavior and actions fearlessly back to love, truth, faith and wholeness. Some days the learning feels like a constant back and forth, especially since having my first child in 2015! Other days feel effortlessly aligned.

THE SEEDS OF VIBRANCY AND HEALTH ARE SPREADING

This process continues to change my experience of my life, which continues to change my life, and in turn I continue to change the world in small and some bigger ways. I now look around and see the role I have played in cultivating a robust and growing Farm-to-Table culture in Indianapolis. I see how the four urban farms we operate—as well as several others we helped get started—have changed the landscape, the urban ecology, and opportunities for food access and education, and have created community gathering places.

I see how the Indy Winter Farmers Market has made it possible for farmers and non-food vendors to grow their businesses and start new businesses that contribute to their livelihood and the local workforce and economy. I see how individuals who have participated in one of our education programs have used the experience as a springboard to reach the next steps in their health journey, study or career path, have found space to offer greater compassion and love to themselves and to others, are paying empowerment forward, and are changing their own lives in ways that change the world. I see how the seeds of vibrancy and health are spreading, taking root and thriving in my community in new ways. And, I am grateful.

Laura Henderson-Founder of Growing Places Indy

WHAT CAN YOU DO?

1. Start discussion about how education is more than textbooks.

---

2. Volunteer for an organization with a mission for education.

---

3. Create a scholarship fund for individuals.

---

4. Go back to school yourself.

---

5. Donate and volunteer to organizations that support education.

Section 5 - Kenya

"WE AS WOMEN MUST JOIN HANDS TOGETHER...THE WOMEN OF KENYA, THE WOMEN OF AMERICA, THE WOMEN OF THE WORLD."

Ida Odinga - Former First Lady of Kenya

▲▲▲

Have you ever traveled somewhere and immediately you knew you had a connection with it? A city, a state, a country, a place of sorts that gave you a certain knowledge that this place spoke to you in a special way? Where you felt a new comfort in your own skin? A place that gave you a feeling of rightness, belongingness and connection with the earth, the people, the energy...the vibe?

I've felt like I was truly home in two places in my life. And one of them is Kenya.

I want you to know some of the beautiful women I met in Kenya and hopefully you'll be reminded that we women have an intrinsic nature of compassion that is part of all of us. Women who recognize the needs of the world...women who choose to spend their time on earth creating change and lifting up the needy...women who understand, as many around the world do, that we have in the palm of our hands and the core of our beings, an energy of compassion, collaboration and communication with humanity and the ability to lead the way to brighter futures.

Fifteen years ago, my oldest daughter Jane announced that she absolutely had to go to Kenya to experience it to satisfy her love of nature and animals, and her drive to be a part of realizing the bigger picture of the world. Yet she was frustrated that it cost so much. So, like any mother, I encouraged her to set her goal to go, to set a plan for saving, work the plan and make it happen for herself.

Two years later she had saved her money and was ready to make the trip happen. She invited me to come with her. And I did.

I had never had a desire to go to Kenya. I always thought when I traveled it would be to Greece because I was in love with the Greek mythology I learned in college. And the thought that my first time out of the United States would be to Africa was intimidating. But I wasn't about to miss a chance to take a "life changing" trip with my daughter. I was happy to say yes.

I had no idea how that trip was to change my life on so many levels. We never know where we'll be when something large or seemingly unimportant can affect us in a way that will take us down a path we hadn't even imagined. I love that about life, don't you? It's such an adventure. It's such a grand experience. The energy of life is always humming along, even when we don't realize it. Whether it's God, or spirituality, or an energy we can't quite name, somehow it knows where it's going. We just need to be open to letting it play out.

The rhythms of Kenya became a part of Jane and me. It wasn't the beautiful country or the wildlife—it was the people who touched me the most. I realized that I had to come back, I had to be a part of this country in some positive way. I wanted to offer my basic abilities and skills to the women and children there. The oppression of women was staggering and the resources for children was minimal.

Fifteen years later, I was blessed to take with me my second daughter, Catt, a journalist and TV host. We traveled with film producer Sally Colón-Petree and a crew to help us tell the story of the people we were to meet there.

Women in Africa are guardians of the family; they are in charge of the maintenance of the agriculture and the welfare of the children, providing the nutrition and providing the education (often only at home for girls), and the family planning at a greater level than anywhere else in the developing world. These responsibilities are a heavy burden on women whose socio-economic status is low and access to contraception is unavailable in many areas.

Women are known to grow 80 percent of the food in Africa, yet in many countries they are not able to own the land they farm or get a bank account without their husband's consent. They end up working 15- to 18-hour days, twice as long as men, and they often age prematurely because of their difficult lives.

It's difficult to rise out of the situation. Without contraception, the burdens of work and family continue to grow. And with the responsibilities they hold, any chance for education, even if it were available, would be difficult to access.

Education participation for women in Kenya is biased. A lack of genuine political involvement to ensure that women—and particularly girls—have equal access to education perpetuates the problem. In general, two-thirds of Africa's illiterate are women.

In some areas, things are changing…slowly. Girls are increasingly getting some limited education and the focus of concern is shifting to providing opportunities for girls as well as boys. Yet, dropout rates continue to be high for girls due to pregnancies and child marriages. Although the law in many countries doesn't allow girls under 16 to be married, parents marry their daughters at an early age so they have one less mouth to feed.

TEN WOMEN AND FIVE TEEN GIRLS JOINED TOGETHER

We started from scratch. My co-founder, Sally, had coordinated many trips in the early years of our foundation: she went to India, Serbia, Costa Rica and Uganda…and I followed. But now, I was planning the first global trip. Thank goodness we partnered with Collette Travel. Although they typically don't do customized trips, they have a beautiful heart and their own foundation for helping the world. Together, we created a trip to see the beautiful country, meet women who are leading the way for change and find lasting friendships of our two worlds through understanding cultures, needs and ambitions.

It took me a year to put the trip together. In the end, another opportunity awaited me—the opportunity to meet and travel with 10 like-minded women and five teen girls for an experience that would impact all of our lives.

Just before we left, there was unrest in Somalia. Some were cautioned to stay home. Some were told there is always unrest in Kenya. Some had the attitude that this would be a missed opportunity if they backed out and they simply got on the plane. Our travel company, all along, was watching the news, determining whether to cancel the trip. They were concerned about our safety.

In the end, it appeared safe to go. And off we went, women from California, Florida, Oregon, New York, Indiana, Arizona, Chicago, all with one goal: to meet with and work alongside the women and girls of Africa.

Remarkably, at the last minute, Sally Colón-Petree, a film producer, made the decision to travel with us and bring a videographer to film what eventually became the *Women Like Us* Documentary.

My daughter, Catt, came with us. Already a seasoned traveler, Catt had never been on a trip like ours. It made a deep impression that she will keep forever. As a journalist and TV host on E! News, she came back to the United States and helped produce our documentary. I was now blessed to have had two of my three children join me in Kenya. Not to be excluded, my son, AJ, is leading our next trip.

▼▼▼

▲▲▲

When I met Nancy Noël, an inspirational and international artist whose heart lives in Kenya, I understood exactly what she was expressing to me that first day I met her to talk about her school on Rusinga Island. She and I bonded, agreeing to use our hearts and our hands to do what we could do there. With how much I loved Kenya, I was up for the task. I was honored that I could go back there, now with a foundation and now with a purpose. Here's how Nancy found her way and shared her heart with the school that eventually became The N.A. Noël Preschool.

▼▼▼

Nancy Noël
FOR THE LOVE OF KENYA

> **❝ WHEREVER YOU LOOK THERE IS OPPORTUNITY TO MAKE OUR WORLD A BETTER PLACE. WE JUST NEED TO CHOOSE TO SEE. ❞**

Throughout time I have realized that the most rewarding and inspiring experiences cross my path unexpectedly. Knowing they are not accidental or coincidences, I have found myself drawn to embrace these encounters and seek their purpose. Perhaps they are gentle invitations to stretch myself to improve the lives of others and to believe that I can. My stumbling upon a small rural hut on Rusinga Island, which sits in Lake Victoria near mainland Kenya, proved this to be true.

Inside this tiny thatched-roof hut, no larger than 12' x 12', were 60 young children standing shoulder to shoulder. They sang joyfully in their native Luo dialect as if they were anticipating a visitor. How did they know I would discover them? And how did they embody such genuine happiness despite how much they lacked? The bleak reality is that many were orphans facing infectious diseases that threatened this precious island. I planned my trip to Africa to enjoy a vacation to photograph children to paint. Without a doubt, my purpose was more deeply rooted; I was meant to help these beautiful children.

On this small island, which stretches no more than three miles wide and 10 miles long, the only means of sending a message is by foot. There are no cars or phones, but they have runners (no wonder Kenya is known for their Olympic athletes in distance running). This is how Mrs. Tom, the preschool teacher, was informed of my probable visit. The natives knew I was setting out for a hike on the island, one of Africa's most remote and historic corners. Little did I know I would be greeted by the beautiful sounds of children singing. This hut, the humble beginnings of a preschool, had just opened days earlier. Since I was their first visitor, they wanted to name their school The N.A. Noël Preschool. The honor was mine, as was the desire to offer them a better life.

The fishing village of Rusinga Island depends on the bountiful fruits of the lake for food, trade, and subsistence. They are showered with rich prospects because their island sits on Lake Victoria, the world's second largest freshwater lake. It was named to honor Queen Victoria when British explorer John Hannig Speke first sighted it in 1858. With a shoreline of 3,000 miles touching the coast of three countries, Kenya, Uganda and Tanzania, Lake Victoria supports Africa's largest inland fishery. Today and historically its value is coveted; Luo in Kenya are known to have fought numerous wars with their neighbors for control of this prized natural resource.

MEAGER WAYS OF BEING

For every native who benefits from the fishing industry, there are countless others who struggle to simply survive. Many villagers live in meager shelters, if anything at all. You see small shanties lining the streets made of cardboard boxes, or a one-room hut made of wood, grass and cow dung. Regardless of their dwelling, they are happy to have a place to call home.

Within the family there is a clear pecking order. A brother assumes the responsibility of taking in a sister or other relative who has lost their spouse. This cultural hierarchy can lead to inequalities between genders. Men have a stronghold on women and their bodies. If women resist, they are punished or whipped. Other perpetual cycles of transgression exist, as well. The superstitions looming over this fishing village lead to a state of misconstrued beliefs. If a spouse died of AIDS or showed signs of illness, they sought a cleansing ritual to chase away evil spirits by way of an exorcist.

To create awareness for a better way, the children in the school performed a play to educate the community. The theme emphasized the importance of living more responsibly and to not be shameful. I am very proud to have these teachers and students openly address these tough issues. By educating and promoting better practices, my hope is to shape better days for these people.

The children are vibrant with laughter and kindness. When in their presence, one sees they are beyond thankful for even the smallest of favors. A piece of candy in my pocket is never grabbed. Instead, they keep splitting the candy again and again until each has a share. They are different from children of other cultures. They are quiet and they listen intently. The N.A. Noël Preschool allows their parents to work—if they have parents.

BRINGING RESOURCES TO THE SCHOOL

Being the sole financial supporter for the school, I quickly learned lessons from which to draw upon. Maintaining the natural rhythm of a given course is very important. Infusing large sums of money causes disruptions and loss of focus. Starting small and growing incrementally allowed the school to evolve more smoothly and efficiently.

Getting money to the children, however, was difficult. Without banks in the area to wire funds to, I sent cash tucked into books and clothing. Unfortunately, the money never reached the school. No matter how well I hid the money, thieves always found it. It was stolen, most likely, when the contents were searched during inspections. It was impossible to avoid this fate.

Theft within the postal service did not discriminate. They not only stole cash, they stole everything. At Christmastime, 2008, I was blessed to have a fine clothier donate more than $10,000 of beautiful clothing, gorgeous sweaters, backpacks, tools and other gifts to my school. Unfortunately, very little reached the children; more than 75% of it was stolen.

Change was necessary if progress was to prevail. And it did. We now have a bank account, which ensures money I send will benefit the children. I no longer need to tuck cash in clothing and fear it will be stolen. Although money reached the school more readily, I was again reminded of the lesson I learned: Do not give too much too quickly. In Nairobi, where supplies were more abundant, kids were snorting glue to get high. This was heartbreaking. You can't give too much, or it exacerbates the problem. Providing a steady, modest amount of aid is how it must be done. Otherwise, our matron would be at risk if it were known she had access to large sums of money.

One of the most successful projects came about when I witnessed malnutrition among the children who showed signs of ringworm, rickets and upper respiratory infections. I contracted a doctor who visits the school weekly to treat the children. As a result of consistent medical attention, the children and their families began to flourish.

The school quickly grew from a half-day to a full-day program. It now cares for 250 children and continues to grow. The school has three classrooms and a playground (which are in a fenced-in property), a host of volunteers, several teachers, a new computer with Internet access, an established bank account and access to supplies.

Never losing sight of our goal, a larger school was built, allowing us to serve more students. Playground equipment arrived so the children could play freely in their new fenced-in area. How excited they were to have such basic amenities as a jump rope and ball. Yellow T-shirts and red shorts became their new uniform, which they wear with great pride.

Many of our supplies came from Nairobi, the capital and largest city in Kenya. This is where we had our uniform T-shirt printed. Nairobi is approximately 200 miles from Rusinga Island; journeying back and forth was typically by a small puddle-jumper. Purchases would often include blackboards, crayons and candy—without wrappers. I am always conscious of eliminating the temptation to litter.

COMMITTED TO CHANGE

The small thatched-roof hut, which I stumbled upon 10 years prior, still stands and functions as our office. Adjacent are three large classrooms where several trained and nurturing teachers serve and educate our students. Nutritious meals are provided daily, newly installed latrines lend dignity and improved sanitary conditions.

I am most happy for the faith I have in the staff running my school, which has emerged from a preschool to an elementary, and the many volunteers who work closely at their side. They chose to be there. I did not entice them with material means; they were already giving of themselves when I met them. My school serves a great need. The N.A. Noël Preschool was the only preschool on the island at that time. In the beginning, the children were between the ages of five and seven (half boys, half girls, and half are orphans. An orphan is a child with one or two parents deceased). Many suffered from AIDS.

Many visitors who come to Africa for the safari experience get caught up in the moment. They see the impoverished rural villages and offer to help; however, follow-through is unusual. Making my word my honor has established mutual trust with my school. These children have been a blessing to me at a level and dimension beyond measure. What we give with a genuine heart always finds its way back to us.

Ever since I was very young, I dreamt of riding elephants in the majestic vast lands. Sometimes I would dream of elephants roaming my back yard, making their way around my swing set. They say, "If you can dream it, you can do it." My travelling to Africa for more than 20 years has allowed me to fulfill my dream. I rode my elephants and I experienced the wondrous beauty of the continent. Being an artist, I wanted to capture the rich tradition of the tribal people on canvas, especially of their dress, with symbolic fabrics and jewelry; my paintings record the culture that otherwise could cease to exist over time. They inspire me to keep their spirit alive when thousands of miles separate us.

When I leave the school to return home, I hear a heart-rending wail—their ritual cry when sadness is in the air. It is a sound that pierces my soul, knowing I will be missed. Also I will always remember the children calling me "Mum," the British version of Mom.

A sight that will never escape my memory is of the most radiant glow of candles floating about small fishing boats off the shore of my resort. It was magical, enchanting and genius at its finest. The fishermen use the candles to attract insects, which are drawn to light. The fish are then attracted to the insects as a source of food. And the fishermen wait patiently for the fish to claim their bait.

Nancy Noël-International Artist and Humanitarian

▲▲▲

Yes, there is a definite circle of life and sometimes life is not fair. I also know that wherever we look, there is opportunity to create a better place. We just need to choose to see it.

On our first morning at Rusinga Island, I left before the rest of our group to go early to The N.A. Noël School. I wanted to meet the children, feel the rhythm, understand the challenges and hear the voices on my own terms.

Walking through the gate I was greeted by Mrs. Tom, the school founder. She is a robust woman with a beautiful smile and an intelligent demeanor. I was immediately drawn to her energy and her sense of purpose. Eventually, I would be invited into her home in one of the worn and leaning buildings on the grounds where I walked on her dirt floors with occasional broken concrete patches, where she housed the bags of beans, rice and dried millet to feed the children, and where she shared the two rooms with her adult family members and 12 children.

MORNING PORRIDGE

I arrived in time for the early morning millet porridge. The children get one meal a day for sure, and that is found in a plastic cup of porridge. I watched them quietly line up outside the door of the kitchen shed, enter the shed where they eagerly yet patiently waited their turn as I gave them a cup of porridge. Then they seated themselves on the dirt floor and ate what might be the only meal of the day. You see, many of the children cannot afford lunch at the school, so this is why the free porridge is so precious.

FAIZANA BROWN

I watched as the porridge was made in a cast-iron pot on an open fire. It was then that I noticed a beautiful baby sitting on the ground who was apparently the child of the cook. I asked if I could hold her. She was dressed in a T-shirt only. And she easily came to me. "This is Faizana Brown," said her mother to me. "Will you take her? Will you take her to America?"

Faizana's mother had many more children. She lived behind the shed and slept on the ground. Her husband had abandoned her. She was a sister of Mrs. Tom and had been taken in by her.

My heart fluttered and my stomach tightened as I was asked to take her child to America. My first reaction was to say "yes." But, of course, that was an impossibility on many levels. Faizana's mother repeated her question to me many times that day. And the next day. I explained that it was impossible and against the law for me to take the child from her mother.

Faizana held on to me that day…and I held on to her. I think about her often. We travel back to The N.A. Noël Elementary next year and I pray she is there and I can be with her again.

We've worked with Nancy Noël and Mrs. Tom in providing latrines, connecting with a donor who provided tubs to catch rain water and sent money for dried millet, beans and corn; and when we go back this year, I am excited for our volunteers to be taught how to build a garden. Now that the water is in place, we can get donations for seeds and plants. It means so much to help them help themselves. When I told them we were coming, they immediately began digging the ground and building a rudimentary fence. Now we just need to get there in June and get started!

▼▼▼

▲▲▲

Mrs. Tom's passion for and understanding of the importance of education, partnered with her love for children who are underserved, is what makes her dedicated to this school she created. Her personal story of perseverance and dedication to a better life for children in Kenya is inspiring.

▼▼▼

Mrs. Tom
A SCHOOL FOR THE CHILDREN

> **MY MOTHER TRIED TO DISCARD ME AND ABANDONED ME IN THE BUSHES AT BIRTH.**

I was born out of wedlock in Kenya. My mother tried to discard me and abandoned me in the bushes at birth. My life would have ended there if a neighbor had not found me and taken me to my grandmother's house. A few years later my mother married and we moved away to a little town called Kisumu. There were nine in my family; I was my mother's firstborn child. The life of young girls and women in Kenya is often seen as a burden, and certainly that is how I felt in my own childhood.

I grew up quite miserable, as I would term it. I never had the luxury of enjoying parental love, and at times I would spend days without food. I can recall one particular early memory where I had unintentionally forgotten to sharpen a pencil for my sister, and my sister reported to my mother. That day I was beaten and thrown out into the rains at night. I sat outside in the cold and wet while the rest of my family remained inside eating their supper. A kind neighbor took me to his house and that is where I slept until morning. Even now as I think back to that evening, I have a difficult time understanding how a mother could slumber comfortably not knowing where her child lay her head.

I was the happiest in my childhood while I was at school. My teachers and classmates kept my mind distracted from the life I lived at home, a life of abuse that lacked kindness and love. Education is a harbor for many children in Kenya, and it was, quite honestly, my own place of refuge. Even as a child I understood that education would be good for me, and I innately knew it was my one path to a better life.

Receiving my education and the ability to attend school, however, was through God's mercy alone. I joined nursery school at the age of four, went to primary school from first to seventh grade, Highway Primary School for eighth grade, and Kisumu Girls High School. My teacher could see I was bright and knew my passion for schooling, so whenever I was sent home for lack of funds and inability to pay the school fees, she would hide me in the classroom without the knowledge of the authorities.

After finishing high school, I met my husband, Mr. Tom. I felt that being away from the home in which I was raised could bring positive change in my life, so together we moved to the town of Rusinga. In this town, the teachers of Dr. Williams School asked me to help them handle and care for the nursery class. That is where I began my journey of giving back to the little ones, and where I taught for two years. It was at that time when I began developing a plan to start my own school for the innocent children within the area living in unfortunate and distressing circumstances. I felt passion in supporting children with backgrounds of poverty, to reach the children who had been abandoned and orphaned. It became my mission to help those children who came from situations much like my own childhood, and those who lacked guidance or a place to go. With the help of international artist Nancy Noël, I opened The

N.A. Noël Preschool in the year 2000, in a small building on the edge of Lake Victoria.

The N.A. Noël Elementary currently accommodates over 200 children. There have been as many as 275. The children arrive to be taken in almost daily and the school continues to grow. We have a doctor who visits the children every two weeks. If any child falls sick with illness at any time, the doctor is called in to treat the child. We also offer uniforms for those who have been orphaned. We are currently working on enhancing our supplies with food and materials. The children take breakfast, which is a mixture of millet and cassava flour made into porridge with a little sugar in it. The noon meal is rice and beans, which is taken twice a week. We have 185 students who go without lunch every day. We have textbooks, but very few of the children can take them home because they are being shared. Our efforts are bringing support and aid by educating and feeding these innocent young children, giving them life's necessary provisions, training, skills, hope and direction. But, there is still much work to do.

Mrs. Tom-The N.A. Noël School Matron

▲▲▲

We met Mama Margaret through the Collette Foundation. She's a joyful woman, full of vitality and hope. We wanted to travel to the Kibera Slums where she lives and created her school, meet the children, volunteer and assess how we could support her; but the unrest with the Somalis was too dangerous. She graciously came to us so we could meet and learn about her work. It was a highlight of my life to meet her. And I look forward to being with her and the children on another trip.

Our group was about to get our first understanding of the hardships and the determination of the Tenderfeet School and their founder, Mama Margaret. I asked Mama to share her story.

▼▼▼

Mama Margaret
A PASSION FOR CHILDREN IN KIBERA SLUMS

> ❝ I COULD SEE HOW CHILDREN WERE LIVING; THEY WERE PICKING FOOD OUT OF THE GARBAGE AND WERE LOITERING IN THE STREETS BECAUSE THEY COULD NOT GO TO SCHOOL. ❞

MY MOTHER HAD A HEART FOR VULNERABLE CHILDREN

I was born in the Central part of Kenya, near Muranga, in 1965. We had a small plot of land, about one acre, and we grew tea and picked tea as a family. This is how my family made a living.

My mother had a heart for vulnerable children. She took in three children: one was a girl who lived with an elderly grandfather, and two were living with a single mother who was a drunkard.

The three children were not being taken care of. I grew up with these three children as well as my brothers and sisters. My parents treated them equally with us. My mother was the responsible one; my father was always a drunkard, but he did pay the school fees for the vulnerable children we took in. The two boys staying with us went to high school. The girl went to live with an aunt and got married and never went to high school. It was very difficult to pay all the high school fees, but my mother really struggled and worked hard so we could have that education.

In high school, I wanted to be a nurse, but I didn't pass chemistry on the national exam. I wanted to repeat my final year of high school and try again, but things were bad at home, so it wasn't possible. During high school, I had a loving aunt who wanted me to come visit her in Nairobi during holidays. She said that after high school she could help me secure a job. Things were not going well at home with my father and his drinking, so I moved to Nairobi after high school. That was in 1984.

MOVING TO KIBERA SLUMS

I lived in the Eastlands area of Nairobi, and I got a job selling shoes and went all over Kenya selling them. I met my future husband, Daniel, in Kisii in 1985 while selling shoes. We became friends first. Then later we connected in Nairobi. At that time, I had started selling clothes. He was working at Kenyatta National Hospital. We decided to get married in 1986 and I became a housewife. I was pregnant and was a bit sickly in 1987. We moved to Kibera that year, since rent and everything else was cheaper there. My first daughter Sandra was born after we moved.

Things were difficult for kids in Kibera. I could see how children were living; they were picking food out of the garbage and were loitering in the streets because they could not go to school. I could feel a passion developing. I thought even though we were doing fine and my husband was earning some money, there was someone out there who was suffering.

In 1989 I decided to go back to work, as a cashier at an

electrical shop and also selling electrical accessories. I did this for two years. In 1991, I had my second daughter, Winnie, and stayed home for a while taking care of my daughters. I eventually went back to work as a cashier and other temporary jobs as I could find them. In 1993, my pastor encouraged me to become a teacher.

I SAW SO MANY CHILDREN WHO COULDN'T PAY SCHOOL FEES

At that time, I was teaching in the Sunday School and the pastor could see I had the gift of teaching children. He wanted me to teach Early Childhood Development (preschool) in his school. It was called Soweto Academy. I was the one at the school monitoring the payment of school fees. I saw so many children whose families couldn't pay them, and those students would be sent home. Then I would see those same children loitering in the streets. Their parents and guardians wanted their children to be at school, but they didn't have the income.

After being at the school for two years—as early as 1994—I realized many of those children were losing parents to HIV/AIDS, and those children were left as orphans. This was especially hard in tribes like Luo, who comprised about 90 percent of the people in the area. In that tribe, if a man's brother dies, he inherits his brother's wife. That's how HIV spread, like a burning bush. At that time, there was no knowledge about the disease and a lot of stigmatization. They were calling it a traditional disease, like a plague or curse. I was asking God, if only I would be able to accommodate two or three of the suffering children, I could offer them education.

In 1995, I had my third child, Samantha. After she was born, I joined another school called Three Bells. I was still untrained, but I now had gained experience as a teacher.

In those days, there were no problems between tribes. Everyone got along, and we loved one another. If I didn't have something, like cooking oil, I could knock at my neighbors' and

I would have cooking oil. Life continued like that and everyone shared. People were socializing and there was no hostility between Luos and Kikuyus (I am Kikuyu). All my neighbors were Luos.

At Three Bells, from 1996-1999, the owner was harsh and would not accept any child who could not pay school fees. If children were sent home, they would never return. At that point, my passion was growing day by day. I made up my mind that one day I would get out of that school and have my own school that would accommodate those vulnerable children who could not afford educations otherwise.

I STARTED TENDERFEET WITHOUT A SHILLING IN MY POCKET

In the year 2000, I started Tenderfeet without a shilling in my pocket. It was located in a KAG (Kenya Assemblies of God) church hall. They were charging 2,000 shillings per month, which was very cheap for rent, but more than I had. I wasn't a member of the church, but some people knew me as a teacher and advocated for me. One of the sets of parents from Three Bells wanted their child to continue being taught by me, and they insisted that they pay my new school what they were paying at Three Bells. I was able to use that money to pay rent, get supplies and start with 10 children. Only one family was paying, the one who came over from Three Bells. I found someone to help in the school, and we worked well together. I continued like that and after one month, we had 25 children, with 10 paying small school fees.

I taught there for three years, until the church was demolished. At that point I had 65 students. We were teaching the three years of pre-primary. In 2002, my brother-in-law helped with the costs of moving into a different building. He provided 27,000 shillings. My brother-in-law had that heart for assisting; he would come and visit and he would see what we were doing. He had that compassion and that love to assist those children in whatever way he could.

In 2003, Kenya began free primary education. Though there were no school fees, families still had to pay for books and uniforms, which was too expensive for many families in the slum. By 2004, I had approximately 100 students. In 2005, my son Ezra was born.

Things were going well with my brother-in-law paying for the school's rent every month. That was until December 2005, when my brother-in-law died in a tragic traffic accident. Without his support, the school was in big trouble.

It was at that time the Lahash group (a non-profit) first visited from the U.S. They said they would advocate for the school. Soon after that, the owner of the building lost patience and we were kicked out and moved to an ACK (Anglican Church of Kenya) church. We were kicked out of there at the end of the year 2006 by the church council.

It was at that time, in 2006, we had a student named Shadrack. He was an orphan living with his aunt and was very sick due to a brain abscess. We were told he had to have surgery. The situation seemed hopeless, but then donors from the U.S., through Lahash, began helping pay for Shadrack's medical bills, such as a CAT scan and other tests. We were forced to move the school to another location, to the Christian Harvest Church. During this time, Shadrack had a successful brain surgery, in March 2007, but his family abandoned him while he was in the hospital, so when he got out of the hospital, he came and lived with my family.

Tenderfeet was soon kicked out of Christian Harvest because they wanted to start their own school, and we had to find another place again. At last, in June of 2007, we were able to find a first real home for the school. It was in a sheet-metal building in a scrap yard, but at least we were not in danger of being evicted. By that time, we had three years of pre-primary and classes one, two and three.

In late 2007, my father was killed. Even though he wasn't

a responsible parent and was a drunkard, I was very much affected. He treated my mother well and they never quarreled, even when he was drunk. He was 100 meters from our home when he was killed by thugs as he returned from the pub.

An election took place in December 2007, and after that there was post-election violence in January 2008. Many Luos were looting, killing, burning houses and rioting. There was chaos all over. The neighbors were shouting throughout the night that they would burn the houses of all Kikuyus. The next morning, I left very early because I felt there was no security. The post-election riots were bad for everyone; countless families were displaced. Many families were assisted during this time through donations, in order to help them find a new home.

Soon after, we relocated to the Riruta area. We got a house and moved in. For two years, we had to have two locations for the school. One school was located in Kibera, for the students who remained there, and one in Riruta, for those who lost their homes and moved to that area. In 2009, we eventually were able to purchase land for a school through the Collette Foundation. Our first classroom building was constructed in June of 2010, and we began having all classes there. At first we rented a school bus, but eventually we were able to purchase an old, used bus and we transported all the children from both areas.

I AM THANKFUL

Five years later, we have five classroom buildings and are able to teach kids from ages three to 13. We now have about 160 students and are able to educate children all the way to grade eight. There is also the Kipepeo program to help girls go to high school. The school has come far since it started. There were so many ups and downs. For the first 10 years, we had no permanent home and many times I feared we would have to close the school due to lack of funds. Now we have sponsors from all over the world, and we met the women of the Women Like Us Foundation in 2014. However, I had to come to them and they could not see the children. There was much unrest in Kenya, so travel to the school was impossible. Our supporters have made it possible to educate these vulnerable children who would not be in school otherwise.

I am thankful to provide the help and education for these beautiful children.

Mama Margaret Wanjiku Nyabuto-Founder of
Tenderfeet School

▲▲▲

Meeting Mama Margaret was inspiring. She set the example and the bar for the wonderful women we were to meet and gave us an understanding of the challenges and strengths of her work in Kenya.

We had arranged to meet Ann Kabui at a specific location in Nakuru. We were at the end of our trip and feeling pretty tired. Travel in Kenya by vehicle is hard. If you've been, you know. Some days we would spend as many as six hours traveling over difficult roads to reach our destination. This was one of those days.

When we climbed out of our vehicle, there before us stood two gracious and enthusiastic women, Ann Kabui and Beth Mwangi. They had been waiting for us. We were happy to meet each other in person after the long process of seeking them out, contacting them from across the world, and traveling thousands of miles to meet them.

I was immediately impressed with Ann's demeanor. She stood proud and confident and with intense eyes that met mine. She meant business.

And Beth, who had connected me with Ann, was proud to be a part of the initiatives that partnered with Ann. They both realized that you cannot reach the children if you don't have the involvement and trust of the mothers. So they partnered. Ann works with the children and Beth established work projects and programs to help women provide for their families and set examples for their children.

When I asked Ann how far it was to the school, she said, "not very far." I was about to learn that not very far has a different meaning in rural Kenya than it does in my world. Ann got back in their car and we followed them down a dirt road to the school. It was located in an area called Njoro, near the Rift Valley. We were unaware that she was bringing us to meet teenagers who had never met an American. I was unaware that this next phase of our trip was to be, for me, an eye-opening experience to the needs of girls and boys in Kenya and the innate goodness and intensity of the women who took on changing their lives through health information and education in school.

Two hours later we arrived at the "not very far" location. Our road to get there was muddy and bumpy. When we arrived at the school, the children greeted us with so much love. They touched our skin. They touched our hair. They greeted us with excitement. They had planned an entire program of presentations, dancing and information. We were honored to be with them. And at the end, we broke into groups and helped our teens from America have time with the teens from Kenya. Although the language was different in this rural place, the connections were made. Questions were asked and interpreted, like "How much do you study?" "What do you do for fun?" "How many brothers and sisters do you have?" And, "Do you know who Beyoncé is?"…at which time they all began singing a Beyoncé song.

It was a memorable time for all of us.

▼▼▼

▲▲▲

Ann Kabui. What a determined, bright and passionate woman. She knows what needs to be done to make a difference for teens in Kenya. From resources for jobs, hygiene initiatives and involving the mothers in the projects, Ann works hard to make a difference. And she doesn't just show up at one school, she shows up at many. Her outreach is growing.
Here's how she began and where she's headed.

▼▼▼

Ann Kabui
TOUCHING THE LIVES OF TEENS IN KENYA

> ❝ A WHOLE GENERATON WAS BEING DESTROYED BECAUSE OF SANITARY TOWELS. I COULD NOT LIVE WITH IT ANYMORE. ❞

I am Ann Kabui. I am passionate about teenagers, and I am the founder of Victorious Teens Bridge International.

I was born in a village called Kagumo in Subukia, Kenya. Although still a young mother, I felt deep love for education and for teenagers' growth and development in marginalized schools. Even before I was married I felt joy by supporting needy teenagers in poor schools and felt inspired by their resilience, despite the challenges most teens faced in my small village.

The changing society in Kenya has also brought about serious challenges to teens. Family break-ups, single parenthood, absentee parents and the lack of extended family leave today's youth with very few resources or mentors with whom to share their problems. As teens grow to adulthood they are ill-advised and uncared-for, lonely and mostly dependent on their peers for decision making.

Persistent absenteeism from school among girls due to lack of sanitary supplies is adversely affecting their education. Because of this, they are susceptible to actions that leave them affected for life. And it is for this reason that I felt obligated and still do feel obligated to make a difference in their lives.

And so I became the founder of Victorious Teens Bridge International, a teens' non-profit organization in East Africa, Nakuru-Kenya. I started the organization in 2010 alongside other volunteers after quitting my job as a banker. Through my passion and commitment to serve and touch lives of needy teenagers in marginalized schools, the organization has provided sanitary towels, undergarments and sports equipment.

Working with donors, partners and well-wishers, the organization has assisted a number of schools like Tayari Secondary School in Molo; Teret Primary School in Njoro, Kipetnden Primary School—sponsored by the Women Like Us Foundation in the United States, Olasiti Secondary School in Nairobi, and I Narok, among others.

As with many teenagers, dating and unhealthy relationships among them remains a concern in both primary and secondary schools in Kenya. Our programs also offer psychosocial support, information on sexual and reproductive health, and counseling.

CHANGING A GIRL'S LIFE WITH SANITARY TOWELS

When I visited several schools in the Nakuru Town West area to plant trees, I was shocked when the girls chose to confide in me about something they cited as "sacred." I was approached by the young girls who explained to me that the unavailability of sanitary towels had forced some of them to resort to the weirdest items to hide their shame.

They used skins, old exercise book pages, feathers, cotton, wool, and in extreme cases, old rags. It hurt me to the core.

"Sometimes we cut our beddings and use them as an alternative means of sanitary towels," claimed one of the students. I could not imagine how something so cheap would be a main problem for the girls to access.

I distributed a couple of the towels I had carried for my own use to the girls, promising I would try to find a solution to the problem. With just three pads, I founded the Victorious Teens Bridge International to oversee the distribution of the towels and that's how I started.

I would lobby for organizations to come and help the young ladies with the much-needed towels, especially after realizing many girls had dropped out of school since they could not face the embarrassment of blood leaking in their skirts. This was, I revealed, one of the main causes of the early marriages, as girls got married to stop the leaks—even though for nine months only.

A whole generation was being destroyed because of sanitary towels. I could not live with it anymore. I was also bitter that no one would create time to talk to the girls and explain to them the changes that were taking place in their bodies.

MY OUTREACH TO SEVEN SCHOOLS IN KENYA

Currently, I support seven schools in Molo, Narok, Nakuru and Njoro. Some students have completed high school and they are helping change the lives of the less fortunate, just as we did for them.

I visit the schools to give moral support to the students and to offer them the much-needed inner-wear and towels.
I target mainly the informal settlements. It's hard for a parent to decide whether she would buy a packet of flour or sanitary towels.

My campaigns have yielded fruits, although with a lot of ups and downs. I still find the strength to continue. I can now distribute the sanitary towels to many girls. I have reached more than 3,000 girls since I started in 2010 and I intend to reach more.

Let me say that I had a burden to help the children in the area, who are mainly abandoned due to the drinking patterns of the parents or being born out of wedlock. Resource mobilization in the area has been a great challenge, especially to convince some companies to come on board.

I have to explain to various people that we have to get inner-wear, as the girls cannot use the tattered ones. I also have to encourage them to buy inner-wear for the boys who need to undergo hygiene classes before we hand them over to them.

I seek to have a country where no one will dread having her periods. It's one of the natural events that happen to girls and should not keep them from getting an education.

CHANGING THE LIVES OF TEENS AND MOTHERS

In 2015, the INVEST IN TEENS program took students from Teret Primary School, alongside their mothers, for a bus trip to Nairobi, the capital city of Kenya. The objective of this trip was to expose them to other environments, to expand their minds and to make them see how much life has to offer. To challenge them and inspire them to know that life is not just what they experience, but that it can be fulfilling, also. It was also to encourage the parents that they, too, can do something to change their lives and the lives of their children.

The visit to Bomas of Kenya, a cultural and learning centre, was also a nice experience for these children. They learned about job creation and talent development, as well as finding alternative sources of income for a better life. This trip was supported by the Women Like Us Foundation based in the U.S.A.

"...this program will always change the lives of our children, just like it's changing our lives at this old age. How I wish during my teenage years I'd had such an opportunity," said one of the mothers.

She is one of the beneficiaries from the Jiendeleze Women's Group, a Victorious Teen Bridge Program that empowers women for sustainable livelihoods. "Jiendeleze" is a Swahili word that means "growth," and it's a program that brings women from marginalized areas together to change their lives through table banking and agribusiness.

Through table banking groups, these women have acquired loans that have enabled them to begin some income-generating activities like poultry and rabbit keeping. Victorious Teens always keeps track and makes frequent visits to see how these projects are doing. We help provide technical skills to these women and link them with potential markets for their products and services. At the end of the day, the program's objective is to ensure that their lives are improved, and that the teenagers are kept in school.

It is clear to me that parents have the responsibility to be a role model for young people. They have a role to play in ensuring a successful life for their children. I believe that an empowered woman will change her family, her community, and her nation at large. We have helped place many of our teen mothers into this program so they can sustain their families.

Through this journey, I have faced a lot of challenges and disappointments, including empty promises from supporters and the pull-out of some stakeholders and donors. But I continue to persevere despite times when all seems lost. I find strength from my team members who are driven by a common goal and vision.

Victorious Teens, just like many other organizations, faces its own challenges, including inconsistent funds to implement its projects. However, we remain thankful for all our partners, well-wishers and donors in and across the region.

As the number of needy teenagers keeps on rising in Kenya, so should be the efforts, linkages and networks. We have always furthered our mission by inviting people, partners and donors to share and support the needs of teens to continue with their education.

Our beliefs and religions may be different, but our challenges are common. Our vision is to empower and nurture teenagers and women in need and help them become responsible Kenyans. Against all odds, we will never get tired of trying. We will never forget that our mission is valid.

Ann Kabui-Founder of Victorious Teens Bridge International

▲▲▲

Beth Mwangi started as a community coordinator in Kenya. It was working with individuals who had fled from post election strife to the Central Rift Valley that she found her passion for helping others. And when she discovered that she could help women by teaching them to raise rabbits, goats and chickens, then sell them to local restaurants, that she knew she could help entire communities in a way bigger than ever before.

▼▼▼

Beth Mwangi
EMPOWERING WOMEN IN RURAL KENYA

> ❝ I REALIZED SHE ONLY HAD FIVE HENS AND HAD FOUR TRAYS OF EGGS. ❞

THE BEGINNING OF MY JOURNEY AS A COMMUNITY COORDINATOR IN KENYA

In 1963 Kenya gained independence. The first president, Mzee Jomo Kenyatta, from the Kikuyu culture, reined until 1978. After Kenyatta died, Daniel arap Moi became the second president. He was a Kalenjin. The Kenyan country is the home of 42 tribes, all of which have different languages and various cultural norms. The country was under a single party until the year 1992 when the introduction of the multiparty system brought a change and a new freedom. This was the year that the Kenyan people began to have rights and the ability to vote for their president, which was, and still is, highly influenced by the tribe. Since 1982 Kenya has been experiencing tribal clashes, especially around the times of these elections. These battles are mostly attributed to the politicians and the lack of employment for the youth, who are the biggest demographic. In each election, four major tribes fight to be represented, and for the presidential seat. During the 2007 election, after the new president was announced, post-election violence ensued. The Kenyan people began horrific fighting with tremendously destructive tribal warfare. Tragically, many people became displaced, their houses either burned down or destroyed, and many Kenyan people lost their lives. This was the beginning of my journey as a community coordinator.

I HAD A GROWING DESIRE TO ENSURE THAT WOMEN WERE EMPOWERED

My first assignment was to help three organizations: Heart to Heart, Black Sheep Women's Group, and NAWAMU IDP Camp (Internally Displaced People). When I first met the groups they were making handcrafts and selling them to tourists, who would either camp in Mwariki or Lake Nakuru Lodge. As a community coordinator in Kenya, my involvement included working closely with the community and the partners (donors). I was based in Central Rift Valley but worked as far away as Nyanza County. During my six years there, I was involved mostly in working with women and children. Most women in developing countries have limited rights compared to developed countries. Being a woman, I knew it was not going to be easy, but I had a growing desire to ensure that women were empowered, just like men.

Working in Nakuru was full of challenges, especially since it's located in Central Rift Valley. Most people who have been affected by the post-election violence have settled in this area. I was required to interact with different tribes and exercise the highest code of ethics without bias or favoritism. Working with these three groups was great exposure for me. We educated the people about micro projects for a source of income, and about financial saving. During community meetings I would often raise issues related to tribalism to help bring understanding about the importance of each person's role within the community. After five years, one of my greatest achievements was bringing the people together, regardless of their tribal descent.

I REALIZED SHE ONLY HAD FIVE HENS AND HAD FOUR TRAYS OF EGGS

Initially, meetings were held every Monday to teach skills for obtaining finances. Every woman was supposed to contribute one Kenyan shilling ($1) each month. One day, during our meeting, one member raised an important question, whether Lake Nakuru Lodge would be interested in buying her eggs to enable her to make a living. Being employed by the lodge, I went to the director (who also works toward empowering women) and discussed the proposition. He agreed, but with hesitation and with questions. "Would she be able to maintain consistency every week?" I went back to the group and discussed it with her and the other women in her home. I realized she only had five hens and had four trays of eggs. She wouldn't be able to supply the lodge with the four trays every Monday. The next time we had a meeting, I had come up with an idea that together the group could rear the hens and together they could create a substantial business.

Soon after, we faced the reality of the economic circumstances. We simply didn't have the capital needed. Regardless of the tribe's initiative to sell the fair trade items, they were not saving and didn't even have a bank account. When we went back to the drawing board, we agreed that the money they had contributed for the two months would be used to open an account. We opened an account, and every month every woman would be saving two shillings minimum and would be given a book to fill her contribution. After six months one would qualify for a loan three times the money she had saved. This was to motivate the women to save more from the sales of handcrafts, rather than spending without a budget.

By the end of my six years, if there's anything I am proud of, it is the change in these women and the NAWAMU community. Through my tenure as a community coordinator, we were able to build a clinic, three classrooms, and houses for the women in the Mbita tribe, and we raised the standard of living of women in the Mwariki and NAWAMU communities.

OUR HEARTS WERE FOR TEENS

One day while I was attending my normal duties, my director, Joseph Muya, introduced me to an organization called Panda Pata. This was when I met Ann Kubui, who is currently the director of Victorious Teens Bridge. During our visit, Ann and I realized we had the same interests in empowering the community—most especially, we had a heart for teens. We had both endured difficult childhoods and understood the challenges the youth faced during their critical adolescent years. We felt it our mission to give back. Ann registered the NGO (Victorious Teens Bridge) and I continued supporting her, especially in the field work. We began fundraising in an effort to support and grow the organization.

As Victorious Teens Bridge developed, various issues were brought to our attention. We recognized that the female children were missing school due to a lack of sanitary towels and undergarments. This absenteeism led to dropouts, drug abuse, early marriages and prostitution. Unfortunately, we became aware of certain circumstances of female genital mutilation, as well. Together, Ann and I began raising the funds to provide sanitary towels, undergarments, and sports equipment. Bringing in the supplies not only assisted in monetary needs, but it also helped bring the community together. It provided an environment of respect, acceptance, and skill development to children in marginalized areas. The Victorious Teens Bridge made a mission to support school education, trips for career exposure, and supplies necessary to help the children rise above their circumstances. Our objective was to inform, empower and nurture the underserved teenagers toward self-realization, and to foster development for future leadership within their communities.

VICTORIOUS TEENS UNITED WITH THE WOMEN LIKE US FOUNDATION

It was during my work with Victorious Teens when I met the Women Like Us Foundation and the director, Linda Rendleman. The Women Like Us Foundation has been a tremendous support in helping Victorious Teens raise funds and supplies to help the underserved teens learn, grow and overcome. The foundation has helped in our efforts to develop a critical program called Beyond the Classroom, building skills and assisting teens in their educational growth. Through the Beyond the Classroom program, we give students the opportunity to visit the city, providing exposure for career opportunities. With the supplies, funds, exposure and education, it is our goal to build a community that is self-reliant and with economic stability.

MY CALL HELPING WOMEN AND TEENS BECOME SELF-RELIANT

We all have different potential. We all can make a difference! If you are a woman or man who has the heart and compassion for helping others in developing countries to become self-reliant, do not hesitate to support them. Your support may be through monetary contribution, traveling the miles to share and encourage them, volunteering in skills development, or donating sanitary supplies, undergarments, toothpaste and toothbrushes, and medical supplies for these marginalized communities. Creating the best future for these children and women will put us one step closer in making this world a better place.

Beth Mwangi-Community Coordinator

FEMALE GENITAL MUTILATION

The most beautiful, lilting, angelic voices I have ever heard came from 25 little girls at the Olmalaika Home in Sekenani, Kenya. The music touched my heart and the look on the faces of the 18 women and girls who traveled to Kenya with me told me they were sure not to forget, either. This was our first true experience of being "on the ground" in support of women who are standing strongly for change in Africa.

The girls at the Olmalaika Home have either run away before or have been rescued after the ritual of female genital mutilation and the threat of early childhood marriage. Their ages range from five to 18, and they all live together in a safe, clean building they call home. The shining eyes and beautiful smiles and the gentle and welcoming demeanor disguised the atrocious abuse they had experienced.

Female genital mutilation is a custom that takes place in many countries, not just Kenya. And it's also practiced in the United States. According to Equality Now, 513,000 women and girls across the U.S. are at risk of undergoing FGM and 26 out of 50 U.S. states do not have laws against it.

> *FGM is the practice of the partial or total removal of the external female genitalia or other injury to the female genital organs for non-medical reasons. This practice is incredibly painful and traumatizing. It can cause death. In Kenya, approximately three million girls mostly under age 15 endure this practice each year.* -Huffington Post

In *Infidel*, the acclaimed book by Ayaan Hirsi Ali, author, politician and activist against female genital mutilation, and who experienced her own cutting at five years old, she explains the process.

"In Somalia, like many countries in the Middle East and Kenya, little girls are made pure by having their genitals cut out. It typically happens around age five. After the child's clitoris and labia are carved out, scraped off, the whole area is often sewn up so that a thick band of tissue forms a chastity belt made of the girl's own scarred flesh. A small hole is carefully situated to permit a thin flow of urine. Only great force can tear the scar tissue wider, for sex.

Held down by her grandmother and two other women… the man picked up a pair of scissors. With the other hand, he caught hold of the place between my legs and starting tweaking it, like Grandma milking a goat. Then the scissors went down between my legs and the man cut off my inner labia and the clitoris. I heard it, like a butcher snipping the fat off a piece of meat. A piercing pain shot up between my legs, indescribable, and I howled. Then came the sewing: the long, blunt needle clumsily pushed into my bleeding outer labia, against my loud and anguished protests. When the sewing was finished, the man cut the thread off with his teeth."

The tearing of the scar is typically done on the wedding night by the husband. This is proof of the purity of the bride.

MEETING FAITH

Her name was Faith. She was a victim of FGM. Our group met her along with 25 girls ages five to 17 at the Olmalaika Home in the Maasai Mara. This home was founded by an amazing American woman, Kim DeWitt. Her perseverance and steadfastness in the fight against female genital mutilation in Kenya has raised greater awareness of this practice and saved the lives of girls.

The way Kim explained it to us, the girls come to her home by running away from the procedure when it is about to happen, or fleeing once it has been performed on them. FGM is a ritual to prepare a girl for marriage. The belief is that the girl will not be clean or ready to be a wife unless she is mutilated. Once married, depending on the type of practice, and, if indeed the vagina is sewn shut, a common part of the procedure, the husband knows she is pure. This practice happens to girls as young as five years old who are soon to be married off and occasionally even to elders.

Faith, tall and lean, with shining determined eyes and an air of quiet strength, had undergone FGM and escaped to the Olmalaika Home. Faith agreed to let us interview her for our film. The interview made us cry for her, yet at the same time we marveled at her strength. She told us she wants to get an education and become a doctor. She wants to come back to help her tribe eradicate the practice.

▼▼▼

▲▲▲

Kim DeWitt. A woman of strong faith, determination and a clear vision of her work in the world. She lived in Kenya as a child and never forgot the needs there. Kim's introduction to FGM at a young age prepared her for her life's work. She's making a difference and creating positive change for girls in Kenya. I'm proud to know her and work with her for the initiatives there.

▼▼▼

Kim DeWitt

MAKING A DIFFERENCE FOR VICTIMS OF FEMALE GENITAL MUTILATION

> ❝ AS A CHILD I HAD BEEN EXPOSED TO THE WAYS OF THE MAASAI TRIBE. ❞

It was July 1966. My eyes literally sparkled with excitement as we boarded the train from Detroit to New Orleans. My grandparents' eyes filled with tears as they waved goodbye to us. I was two years old, and for them it would be five long years until they would see us again. Once we reached New Orleans our trunks and barrels were loaded onto a huge ocean liner called the Helen Lykes. I held my mum's hand as we climbed up the steep gangplank. The whistle blasted as the tugboat led us down the Mississippi River into the Gulf of Mexico and on, out into the deep blue Atlantic Ocean. Four weeks later we arrived in Capetown, South Africa.

About a month later we boarded another ship called the Kalahari. The railings along the deck were not made with mesh like on the other ship. Over the next five weeks I would spend my time gripping the railing with my little hands and swinging out over the turquoise blue waters of the Indian Ocean, watching the seagulls fly by and waving at the workers on the wharf whenever we docked at a port along the eastern coast of Africa.

At last we sailed into the port of Mombasa: we had arrived in Kenya! From the port, we were taken to the depot where we loaded everything on the train and slowly chugged along through Tsavo National Park on our way to Nairobi. Giraffes nibbled at the tops of the green Acacia trees, elephants drank from the water reservoirs and hyenas laughed in the darkness. Little did I know that this would be the beginning of an amazing journey, something that would mold and shape my heart, creating in me a passion for Kenya, her people and her wildlife.

I spent my childhood on a farm with dogs, cats, chameleons, ducks, rabbits, a cow that had twins, a spider named Charlie who came out from behind the picture on my wall each night, and a praying mantis that lived in my window between the screen and the glass. I attended Maxwell Preparatory School and learned about Livingston and the explorations of Africa. We celebrated Guy Fawkes Day and Boxing Day, instead of 4th of July and Thanksgiving.

MY LIFE ALTERED IN BEIRUT

After about 12 years of being at home in Kenya, my parents moved us to Beirut, Lebanon. My life changed dramatically. Because of the civil war, we spent a lot of time in bomb shelters and I became accustomed to bullets and rockets whistling by. It was while we lived in Lebanon that I experienced something that would forever alter my life, something so painful that I would tuck the memory away deep inside of me, keeping it a secret for more than 30 years.

Eventually we were evacuated to the Greek island of Cyprus. There was no church school for us to attend, so my brother and

I were sent to an American boarding school in Singapore. Those were some of the hardest years of my life. I was far from home and was the only American student. I looked at life differently than most around me. I never did fit in. I was different.

I realized my heart was African, though my skin color and everything of outward appearance suggested I was American. In my junior year my parents moved back to the United States.

FEELING ON THE OUTSIDE IN AMERICA

Life was very tough, as I had no desire to be in the U.S. There were no warm and fuzzy feelings when it came to Thanksgiving or 4th of July. I did not know the Pledge of Allegiance or the National Anthem, but I could sing the Kenyan one! Those around me talked of movies and TV shows I had never heard of. I spelled words differently than Americans did; they were marked as incorrect, even though they were spelled perfectly right in British schools. There was a lot of adjusting that took place over the following years, and a lot of bitter and hurt feelings. The memory of what had happened in Lebanon still haunted me daily. I longed to go back home to Africa.

In 1999 my husband and I were offered jobs in Kenya. For six years we lived in southern Kenya on the edge of Maasailand. Weekends were spent out in the bush with our Kenyan friends, or camping in the national reserves and parks. My life began to have purpose and meaning again; I began to feel like everything I had gone through as a child was for a purpose.

As a child I had been exposed to the ways of the Maasai tribe—their nomadic, pastoralist lifestyle, polygamy, female genital mutilation (circumcision) on their young girls, and childhood marriage.

They were steeped in tradition and un-wanting of the Western ways that were creeping in around them. I had attended a girls' circumcision ceremony. I remember being separated from my family and led into the center of the women and girls, later being returned with the red ochre painted on my face and beadwork hanging around my neck. I had no idea at that age that all the singing and dancing was really covering up a terrible deed: female genital mutilation.

Years later, I found myself fascinated by the ritual. I wanted and needed to know more to understand it. I began reading articles and books, I talked to Maasai friends, and I even requested to attend a circumcision ceremony to take pictures. It was not long before the harsh reality sunk in.

Hundreds, if not thousands, of little girls all around me were enduring female genital mutilation between the ages of six to 16. My heart filled with an overwhelming desire to make a difference. How could I stand by knowing that it was going on around me and do nothing?

I listened to little girls' stories of how a piece of tin had been sharpened and in the morning hours their legs had been tied and stretched apart, their hands bound so they could not fight back. A small basin of cool water was splashed on their vaginal area and while crying out in pain, their clitoris, labia majora and minora were slowly sliced off. I held a little girl who had escaped—she had watched her sister bleeding to death while her family stood by helplessly. Her heart was gripped with fear and she fled looking for safety, as she knew the family would now turn to her as the next child to be circumcised and married off.

I met little girls who were in the hospital because at the tender age of eight or nine they had been married off to a 62-year-old man, their bodies infected and torn from their husband's desire for sexual intercourse. The young girls I met would stare down at the ground, fearful for their eyes to meet mine. These girls felt ashamed and alone, having trusted in their family who in the end were the very ones forcing them to endure this. Every story I listened to was hauntingly the same. I realized how much in common I had with each little Maasai girl.

Each day of my life, for 30+ years, I had relived my own secret memory that I had hid deep inside of me. I was in seventh grade when a young man, whom my family knew, invited me to go for a walk with him. When we reached a secluded place he forced himself on me. I begged and pleaded to be let go, but my pleas fell on deaf ears. I had never told anyone about it except my husband.

Silently and alone I relived it each day of my life.

FINDING MY PURPOSE WITH VICTIMS OF FGM

Years later during my quiet time one morning, I asked God to help me understand why someone I knew would do what he did to me. It was almost like I heard His voice say to me, "We both have scars; yours cannot be seen from the outside but are deep within you. Mine are in my hands and feet and will always be visible to all. The only difference between our scars is that I chose mine and you did not. I will carry my scars forever, but because of those scars, someday your scars will all be gone!"

There was a peace that came over me. Now when I feel my scars so deep within me, I no longer have to relive my pain, but instead I can praise God for the scars He chose just for me! My scars would pave a path to a lifetime passion of making a difference for young girls facing female genital mutilation and early childhood marriage. In so many ways my life experiences were so very similar to what young Maasai girls face. Someone they knew and trusted forced them to be circumcised, and they often had no one to share their stories with, or they felt too ashamed to tell.

They also carry inner scars; they don't see themselves as valuable.

The Maasai girls in Kenya and girls in general around the world need a voice and someone who can understand them. I knew that the scars I carried enabled me to be a voice for them. There is a home now in Sekenani, Kenya, filled with giggles and hugs coming from 38 little girls.

The Olmalaika Home (Olmalaika meaning "angel"), is a safe haven for young Maasai girls between the ages of five and 12 who are at high risk of female genital mutilation and early childhood marriage. I like to say, "it is a home where little angels dwell."

Kim DeWitt-Founder of Olmalaika Home

WHAT CAN YOU DO?

1. Educate yourself on the rights and needs of women and girls globally.

---

2. Read *Half the Sky* by Nicholas D. Kristof and Sheryl WuDunn.

---

3. Help spread the word about FGM and the fact that it also exists in the U.S.

---

4. Donate to a woman-led organization that is fighting to eradicate FGM.

---

5. Travel and volunteer.

Conclusion

> **"I HAVE IN THE PALMS OF MY HANDS AND THE CORE OF MY BEING, THE ABILITY TO MAKE A DIFFERENCE. AND WHEN WE AS WOMEN DO IT TOGETHER…WE CAN CHANGE THE WORLD."**
>
> Linda Rendleman

▲▲▲

So that's it. It's the end of this book. But it isn't the end, really, is it? In fact, I am hoping that for you it is only the beginning.

Now is only the beginning for you to think deeply about what you can do to live a life that includes action to help the world. It's only the beginning for you to dig deep, discover what thrills you, what makes you understand your purpose, and what motivates you to start taking those first steps toward putting your own personal stamp on the world. And it's only the beginning for you to join us, you, who are a Woman Like Us, just like us, in whatever way it fits for you, as part of the history we are creating for a better world. Whether in your own back yard or across the Earth, there is need. All you need to do is hear what resonates within you and understand how you see your part for the greater good.

In my daughter Catt's introduction, she said it well. For her, she just needed to take the steps…to "get on the plane." Both she and I beckon you to do the same. Step out, step up, step through your life to a whole new level. Get on that metaphorical plane and join the millions of women who are living a fulfilling and purposeful life of intentional giving for a better world.

BIOGRAPHIES

Catt Sadler

Television Host & CEO of #theCATTWALK.com

As an Emmy-winning journalist with years of experience, Catt Sadler is one of the most revered TV hosts in the business. She is renowned for her work on E! News, which spans E! News (role: host), E! News Weekend (role: co-anchor), and a myriad of network specials (role: host). Catt also rocks the red carpet while covering high-caliber events and interviewing celebrities during awards season and New York Fashion Week.

Catt has not only served in the expansion of her TV duties, but has contributed to her own success as the CEO of her own digital lifestyle brand: #theCATTWALK. With a career in the public eye, Catt's personal style has garnered her legions of fans. Her influence is detailed on her wildly popular blog, #theCATTWALK, as well as her other social media platforms. Catt is also a contributor to E!'s Style Collective and she serves as the host and moderator of all Simply Stylist Fashion and Beauty Conferences. Catt has collaborated with a number of high profile brands including Ford, Bvlgari, American Express, Nordstrom, Bausch + Lomb, Murad Skincare, and more.
Catt just completed her role as executive producer on her first documentary, *Women Like Us: Three Women. One Journey. To Change the World*. It is a philanthropic effort to support The Women Like Us Foundation.

Dianne Atkinson Hudson

Producer and Entrepreneur

Dianne A. Hudson has a distinguished record of 30 years as a media executive, writer, producer and entrepreneur.

Dianne received a Bachelor of Arts in broadcast journalism from Ohio University in Athens, Ohio.

She joined Harpo Studios in Chicago in 1986 as a producer. From 1994 to 2003, she was executive producer of the number-one-rated, award-winning *Oprah Winfrey Show*. She has received nine Emmy Awards from the National Academy of Television Arts and Sciences.

During her tenure as executive producer, Dianne is credited with establishing Oprah's Book Club, which has been noted for re-invigorating the commercial book publishing industry.

She also conceptualized and implemented the viewer-driven public charity Oprah's Angel Network, which served to encourage ordinary citizens to use their lives in the highest potential. During The Oprah Winfrey Show's 2000 season, an Angel Network Use Your Life Award of $100,000 was given weekly to viewers who had independently established their own charitable efforts to help others in their communities or throughout the world.

In 2002, viewers contributed over $7 million to Oprah's Angel Network after seeing a special program on the ABC Network and *The Oprah Winfrey Show*, focusing on how the HIV/AIDS crisis in South Africa is affecting that country's children. Dianne was executive producer of a three-week series of events called ChristmasKindness, during which Oprah Winfrey distributed Christmas gifts of toys and clothing to 50,000 children in South Africa. The money raised was used to build schools, buy uniforms and school supplies, and fund organizations that support children orphaned by HIV/AIDS.

Dianne also served as Vice President, Harpo Productions, and

President of The Oprah Winfrey Foundation and Oprah's Angel Network.

As President of The Oprah Winfrey Foundation, Dianne negotiated an agreement with the South African government, and then supervised the building of The Oprah Winfrey Leadership Academy for Girls in South Africa, a world-class boarding school for underprivileged girls in grades seven through 12. The Academy, developed at the request of Nelson Mandela, opened in January 2007.

Currently, her company, Andre Walker Hair, LLC, develops and sells beauty products for women, including the Andre Walker Hair Gold System, with exclusive distribution in all Target Stores, and pending expanded retail distribution.

Nancy D. O'Reilly, PsyD

International Philanthropist
Founder of Women Connect4Good, Inc.

International philanthropist and trailblazer for women empowerment, Nancy D. O'Reilly, PsyD, launched the 501(c)(3) foundation, Women Connect4Good, Inc., which urges women to support each other to create a better world. Her lively, humorous and engaging presentations and memorable events inspire audiences across the country to create satisfying and purposeful lives.

A frequently published author, she originated and co-authored the book *Leading Women: 20 Influential Women Share Their Secrets to Leadership, Business, and Life.*

As a clinical psychologist, Dr. Nancy served as director of a large employee assistance program, and as a Nationally Certified Crisis Team Leader in New York City after 9/11. Through the years she has helped people triumph over devastating trauma from weather disasters, fire, divorce, health crises and job loss. She has earned many honors and awards and serves tirelessly on boards including as Chairman of The Responsibility Foundation Board, leading the fundraising project to build the Statue of Responsibility, which is to be the Pacific Coast symbol of freedom to bookend the Statue of Liberty on the East Coast, supporting Take the Lead's Train the Trainer program, hosting the next session in her home in Santa Barbara and also serving on the governor-appointed Missouri Committee of Psychologists Board of Directors.

Rachel Roy

Designer and Philanthropist
Founder of the Rachel Roy Brand
Founder of Kindness is Always Fashionable

Rachel Roy is the founder of her eponymous brand and a tireless activist for using our voice to encourage change and design the life we want to live. The Rachel Roy brand debuted in 2004 and for over a decade has been inspiring women to lead individual and limitless lives through courage, conviction and change. Rachel has built her ready-to-wear and accessories business into a globally recognized brand with product categories including contemporary, curvy, dresses, outerwear, jewelry and swimwear.

In addition to running her successful brand, Rachel is a sought-after speaker on entrepreneurship and philanthropy, and she has shared her story and experiences at forums ranging from the White House, to Fortune's Most Powerful Women conference series, to other various women's empowerment summits. Rachel nurtures young design talent globally through her work with the Woolmark Prize, Who's Next/Vogue Mexico and CFDA incubator programs.

Rachel has been recognized by the Accessories Council with an ACE Award for best brand launch, and as one of Mattel's 10 Women to Watch, as well as numerous Best Dressed Honors including Vanity Fair's Best Dressed List. She has also been recognized for her innovative brand and film work by AdWeek Media and the La Jolla Fashion Film Festival. She has been a contributing columnist to Huffington Post and *InStyle* magazine.

Rachel founded Kindness Is Always Fashionable as an entrepreneurial philanthropic platform to help women artisans around the world create sustainable income for their families and communities through design projects. Rachel is a member of the Council of Fashion Designers of America.

Patricia Darquea

Founder of ShadyFace

Patricia Darquea was born in California, as the proud daughter of two wonderful Austrian parents who immigrated to the United States from Vienna. Her first language was German/Austrian which led to majoring in broadcasting with a minor in German and international relations from San Francisco State.

KGO Radio and KNTV 11 internships provided the springboard for her public speaking career including commercials and movies. Through her burning desire and dedication to the craft of acting, she earned her union affiliation with Screen Actors Guild (SAG). As a working actor and still in college, she built a makeup and hair business that became extremely successful, while supporting her passion for the arts.

As her public speaking career became more demanding, Patricia realized her passion and expertise was to be a spokeswoman. This direction in her life led to a career in industrial commercials, representing large corporate entities throughout the United States in the technology, medical and automotive industries, at trade shows and conventions.

Patricia is the inventor of the ShadyFace Sunshades Brand and the CEO of a successful international sun protection brand, which has expanded into the pet arena for pet protection.

Patricia is enjoying her journey through life with her husband of 24 years and two rescue dogs, Romeo and Lucci. She gives back to numerous charities as well as rescue facilities for animals.

Sally Colón-Petree

Founder of Dream On Productions

Sally Colón-Petree is a native of Chicago. After attending Oral Roberts University where she studied film and television production, Sally relocated to Los Angeles in 1996 to pursue her career in the entertainment industry. A year after arriving in Los Angeles, Sally landed a role in the dark comedy *Eight Heads in a Duffel Bag*, starring Joe Pesci and David Spade, followed by several guest-starring roles on network television shows and national commercials, as well as landing a coveted spot on the cover of *Woman's World* magazine. In 2001, Sally signed a $1.3 million record deal as part of a Latin girl group managed by Suzanne DePasse, a Motown executive responsible for discovering the Jackson 5. Later, Sally decided to focus on creating family-friendly programs and moved into producing and hosting TV, which included traveling across the country to participate in press junkets for major motion picture companies.

After five years of hosting television, Sally was awarded two Telly awards for her work as a producer and TV host. In 2003, Sally married Stephen Petree, and a year later they started Dream On Productions, a company focused on creating family-friendly TV programming, feature films, documentaries, artist development and management and music composition. Their recording studio and production offices are located in Valencia, CA. Sally is making her directorial debut in her latest project called *Women Like Us: Three Women. One Journey. To Change the World* a humanitarian documentary.

Sally serves on the boards of The Los Angeles Dream Center (an urban outreach center in downtown L.A.), and the Women Like Us Foundation.

Linda Smith

President and Founder of Shared Hope International

Linda Smith is a leader in the global movement to end sex trafficking. In 1998, while serving in the U.S. Congress, Linda traveled to a notorious brothel district in India where the hopeless faces of women and children forced into prostitution compelled Linda to found Shared Hope International in order to support shelter and service creation for sex trafficking survivors using a comprehensive model for restoration. By partnering with local organizations, SHI provides restorative care, shelter, education and job skills training through the Women's Investment Network (WIN) at Homes and Villages of Hope, where women and children can live without time limit. Today, Shared Hope provides leadership in education and training, prevention strategies, research and policy initiatives.

Linda is the primary author of *From Congress to the Brothel* and *Renting Lacy,* and she co-authored *The National Report on Domestic Minor Sex Trafficking* and the *DEMAND Report*. Linda has testified before Congress, presented at national and international forums, and has been published in news outlets and journals. Linda served as a Washington State legislator (1983-93), before she was elected to the U.S. Congress in 1994 as a result of a write-in campaign. Linda and her husband, Vern, reside in Vancouver, Washington. They are the proud parents of two and grandparents of six.

Kyla Smith

Activist

Kyla Smith moved to Los Angeles, California, in April of 2010 to be a full-time volunteer at The Dream Center. Her first position was with Project Hope, a program working with women recovering from human trafficking. Due to her commitment to human trafficking, The Dream Center appointed her to be the director of the program.

As a result of her passion and the needs of the program, Kyla has initiated a street outreach, working long hours into the night to reach the girls who are victims in sex trafficking. She formed a rescue team and opened an emergency shelter specific to trafficked victims. Kyla has also pursued relationships with NGOs, churches, and law enforcement, and with individuals who also focus on assisting trafficked victims. She has obtained certification in interviewing and identifying victims of human trafficking and completed Professional Assault Crisis Training, as well as law enforcement trainings. She has facilitated almost 400 rescues in the last six years.

Kyla is a member of the L.A. Metro Task Force, Orange County Human Trafficking Task Force, Long Beach Human Trafficking Task Force, and ICAN Task Force, as well as the San Diego Human Trafficking CSEC Service Providers Committee. She is a graduate of the spring 2016 class of Homeland Security Citizen Police Academy and a recipient of Vanguard University's Center for Woman and Justice 2015 Diamond Award.

K.D. Roche
Survivor

Over the past eight years, K.D. Roche has volunteered at domestic violence shelters and has trained hotel and hospital employees, as well as community members, on recognizing the signs and red flags of human trafficking. She has helped residential programs with the development of practices and curricula, and trained law enforcement, social workers and medical providers.

The topics K.D. has addressed are many:
- The long-term recovery process for PTSD/CPTSD survivors
- Trafficking in the LGBTQ community (specific needs serving LGBTQ populations and vulnerabilities of LGBTQ youth)
- Rural trafficking
- The importance of implementing services for young male survivors of abuse in preventing human trafficking
- Keeping up with technology (law enforcement training) and how to catch predators *before* they strike
- Grounding techniques when in "fight or flight," common triggers and many more.

K.D.'s story is told in full in the recent book, *Made in the USA*, by Alisa Jordheim. Her story appears in chapter 4 on familial/rural trafficking.

Jessica Evans

Founder of Purchased

Jessica is the Founder of Purchased, an anti-trafficking nonprofit in Indianapolis.

Upon returning from a trip to Nepal in 2007, where her heart was first tugged by the issue of human trafficking, she knew that God had placed a calling on her life to be a part of the abolition movement by educating the community on this issue and inspiring them to join in the fight. She then called on a team of friends to take a journey of faith with her to create an education and awareness campaign that has become Purchased. Since its foundation in 2011, Purchased has been committed to highlighting value and dignity in the girls they have the honor of serving.

Jessica is a 2003 graduate of Indiana Wesleyan University. She previously taught kindergarten and 1st grade in Indianapolis. She recently received a certificate in Nonprofit Executive Leadership from IU. Jessica is currently an active member in the Indiana Protection of Abused and Trafficked Humans (IPATH) task force.

Shaunestte Terrell

Deputy Prosecuting Attorney, Human Trafficking Missing Persons Division – Indianapolis, Indiana

Shaunestte Terrell is a Deputy Prosecuting Attorney at the Marion County Prosecutor's Office, where she is assigned to the Human Trafficking/Missing Persons Unit. She frequently participates in undercover investigations and prostitution ring busts, which she then prosecutes in Marion County Superior Court or refers to the United States District Attorney's Office, where she serves as a consultant.

Prior to serving in the Human Trafficking/Missing Persons Unit, Shaunestte was assigned to the Special Victims Unit, where she prosecuted rape, child molestation and other crimes against protected persons.

When she is not prosecuting, Shaunestte teaches courses in Criminal Justice at Harrison College, and serves on numerous boards, including: the Indiana Protection for Abused and Trafficked Humans Task Force, the Commercially Sexually Exploited Children Working Group, United Way Youth as Resources, Drug Free Marion County, and the Indianapolis Bar Association Criminal Justice Section, where she is the Chair-Elect.

Shaunestte has a long history of public service. Upon graduating with full honors from Purdue University in 2004 with degrees in history and psychology, Shaunestte served in AmeriCorps. During her service, Shaunestte worked for the National AIDS Fund, stationed in Charlotte, NC. As part of her responsibilities, Shaunestte frequently presented in community forums on HIV/AIDS, conducted HIV testing and counseling, and also participated in client services for those living with HIV/AIDS.

Lolly Galvin

Founder, Dignity Project & #phillystreetcuts

Lolly Galvin is the founder of Dignity Project. The organization's goal is to provide essentials to those experiencing homelessness, while also sharing their stories via social media.

She has taken her movement on the road to 14 U.S. cities via The Dignity Tour.

The Dignity Project started from humble beginnings with a GoFundMe campaign and a goal of $500 to do random acts of kindness for the homeless. The goal was reached in three days and she took a homeless man out to lunch. After posting his story, the reaction was overwhelming. Donations poured in and she came up with an idea to hand out "Dignity Bags," which are filled with essential toiletries as well as hand warmers, socks and gloves for those living on the streets of Philadelphia. After reaching $2,000, Lolly proposed a plan via social media to live in a van while traveling cross-country to deliver dignity bags and bring awareness to homelessness in 12 U.S. cities. Again, the response was overwhelming with nearly $7,000 in donations from 170+ people worldwide.

Shaaron Miller Funderburk

Founder and CEO of Off the Streets Program, Inc.

Shaaron is the founder and CEO of Off the Streets, Program, Inc., a 501(c)(3) Female Recovery House in Gaston County. This program provides women the opportunity to recover from alcohol and drug addiction and sexual abuse in a safe and healthy environment. Shaaron provides one-on-one and group counseling to people with HIV/AIDS. She has created a Self-Esteem and Life Skills Program (SEALS) for recovering addicts. She initiated an NA 12-step program in Gaston County and provides supportive community resources. She is currently the liaison of a support group that has been held at First United Methodist Church for 19 years.

Shaaron is a native of Gastonia, North Carolina. Shaaron is very involved in the Gastonia community, where she serves on various boards and committees, including: The Gaston Faith Network, Care Connection, HIV/AIDS Taskforce, Emergency and Transitional Housing, The Mayor's Task Force and Project Homeless Connect, Housing Committee Long Range Planning and Advisory Board, CHIN Committee, GAP committees, and Run for the Money steering committee for 12 years. She served as the Vice-President of the Women's Commission 2006-2008. She also served as the Vice-President of the Forestview High School Band Boosters, 2012-2013.

Shaaron created and implemented the Relationships in Recovery (RIR) support group in 2005 to help women learn how to become healthy in relationships and in the family. RIR is geared toward marriage rather than cohabitation.

Shaaron is married to Rev. Derick Funderburk and has a daughter, Parrisha K. Barnes, who serves in the U.S. Navy and is stationed in Pearl Harbor (Hawaii).

Caroline Barnett

Co-founder of The Dream Center

Born in Sweden, Caroline Olsson moved to the United States at the age of two. In 1996, she visited The Dream Center after hearing her family discuss the tremendous work they were doing for the people within Los Angeles. After her visit, Caroline felt God calling her to volunteer at the Center. At the age of 18, Caroline and her best friend started a program with the Dream Center called the Food Truck Ministry. It was an idea to take food out to the people on the streets daily. Since then, this program has grown into a huge outreach, currently feeding over 50,000 people each month.

Caroline has an amazing heart for all people. She works in The Family Floor, which helps homeless families, and Project Prevention, a foster care program designed to keep families together. Caroline also leads a Women's Ministry. She feels that it is a God-given mandate to inspire women to find their passion to change this world.

In 1999 Caroline married the Dream Center Senior Pastor, Matthew Barnett. Together they have ignited a spark in the inner-city of Los Angeles, California. The Dream Center is currently reaching over 30,000 people every week for the Lord Jesus Christ, providing food, clothing and other necessities.

In 2001 Matthew and Caroline also became the senior pastors of the Angelus Temple, the birthplace of the Foursquare denomination, giving the Dream Center ministry a much needed sanctuary.

The historic Angelus Temple and the Dream Center are reaching large numbers of people in Los Angeles and are truly effecting change in an impoverished area of a hurting city where many believed a large church could never exist at all.

Marie Griffin

Griffin Marketing & PR Founder/President

Marie Griffin is a sought-after authority in media, communication and executive training for leaders in entertainment, fashion, beauty, sports, wellness, publishing, design, finance, technology and politics, among other areas. Her hallmark is her ability to elevate clients to their most authentic and confident selves. Marie's immersive process is informed by a deep knowledge of the media landscape and is described by one notable client as "honest, insightful and transformative."

Marie began her career in front of the camera as a *Seventeen* magazine editor. As U.S. Director of Paris-based think tank Promostyl and VP of Global Marketing and New Business development at pop culture research firm POP-EYE, she spent over a decade branding, marketing and trend forecasting for the world's most valuable brands. In 1995, she launched Griffin Marketing & PR, a media training meets branding and broadcast media PR firm.

Celeste Mergens

Founder and CEO, Days for Girls International

Celeste is the founder and CEO of Days for Girls International (DfGI). Since 2008, Days for Girls has restored days of education and opportunity to over 400,000 women and girls in more than 100 countries in six continents, through providing access to sustainable feminine hygiene solutions and health education. Celeste founded Days for Girls at a time when virtually no other organizations were speaking about the global need for menstrual hygiene management solutions, or the potential for those solutions to help break the cycle of poverty for women. Celeste has led Days for Girls to develop a global network of over 760 volunteer Chapters and Teams, and social enterprise programs in 13 countries, all while maintaining an extremely low overhead.

Celeste was featured as a panelist at the 2015 and 2016 UN Commissions on the Status of Women. Her TEDx video has surpassed 16,000 views. Days for Girls is a two-time Girl Effect Champion, and was named by the Huffington Post as a 'Next Ten' Organization poised to change the world in the next decade. Celeste averages 50+ speaking engagements per year.

She has been featured in *O, The Oprah Magazine, Glamour,* and *Stanford Social Innovation Review*. She is known for her inclusive and empowering leadership. She was 2014's Washington State American Mother of the Year, and a recipient of the Soroptimist Ruby award. Days for Girls was born in an "aha moment," after an event in the slums of Kenya prompted the idea for a simple and sustainable solution to reversing the cycles of poverty and violence for women.

Deborah Myers

Founder of the One Girl at a Time Program

Deb Myers has been on the Women Like Us Foundation board since its inception. She has been instrumental in helping to develop, implement and convey the mission of the Women Like Us Foundation. As national president of the governing board, Deb has led the foundation in building strong partnerships and program mentors. She continues to direct and organize Women Like Us Foundation events, such as the Annual Tea and Speaker Series and Annual Symposium, which have hosted thousands of attendees.

Deb is the National Director and Developer of the Women Like Us Foundation's One Girl at a Time Program, which has impacted thousands of girls while advocating for teens. Deb has doubled her program impact each year and continues to actively participate as a mentor, speaker and workshop leader.

She dedicates herself to the belief that women and girls together can achieve their dreams and change the world. She promotes creating awareness and support for women worldwide. Her message is conveyed through the programs she leads—knowing that as informed, confident women and girls, we can make positive impact in our own lives and in our communities.

Elissa Kravetz

The Farley Project

Elissa Kravetz began her career in PR as a personal intern and muse for shoe industry giant Steve Madden. From intern to Director of PR, Elissa saw this international company through many innovative and far-reaching PR and marketing campaigns during her four-year journey in-house with the company.

In 2002, Elissa joined the high profile lifestyle PR firm People's Revolution, working in their Los Angeles office on a variety of fashion and beauty brands. In 2004, Elissa and a fellow colleague came together and formed the successful lifestyle public relations agency, Spin Shoppe PR. In the three years Elissa was founding partner, she oversaw some incredible high-profile media campaigns including Heatherette, 2 B Free, Steve Madden and Prive Salon. Elissa also spearheaded many special events, including the 2 B Free Fashion Show Presented by Sony Ericcson, the launch of the Palms Hotel and Casino Pool in Las Vegas, Disneyland's 50th Anniversary at Fred Segal Fun, Santa Monica, and many more.

Elissa is the founder of The Farley Project, an anti-bullying non-profit organization dedicated to traveling to camps and middle schools around the country, educating kids, parents and teachers about the effects of bullying.

Laura Henderson

Founding Director of Growing Places Indy

Laura Henderson is the founding director of Growing Places Indy and the Indy Winter Farmers Market, and she is a certified yoga instructor.

Growing Places Indy is an Indianapolis nonprofit that empowers individuals and communities to *Grow Well, Eat Well, Live Well, Be Well*™. The organization cultivates connections between people, food and community through a unique blending of urban agriculture and food access with the art and science of yoga. She designed and directs the Growing Places Indy Summer Apprenticeship Program, which guides aspiring leaders on an in-depth journey of food and community awareness, and personal transformation. Laura currently serves on the board of the Indy Food Council, and previously served for the Indy Food Coop and Butler University Center for Urban Ecology. She has consulted for numerous organizations, public and private projects, and events related to urban agriculture, food matters, sustainability and mindfulness.

Laura teaches yoga at Invoke Studio, is an ambassador for Lululemon Athletica, and serves as a mentor nationally for the Catalyst Collective's yoga-based leadership training program. She has completed a number of trainings in conscious activism, personal development and community leadership with Off the Mat Into the World.

Laura graduated from Butler University in 2000, and completed an international MBA in executive leadership in Europe (Slovenia) in 2014.

Nancy Noël

International Artist

Nancy Noël is an International Artist and Humanitarian. Her art hangs in homes of notable people around the world, including Oprah Winfrey, Jane Seymour and Mikel Gorbachev.

As a little girl playing up in a tree in her back yard, Nancy pretended she was riding an elephant in Africa while most girls were playing with dolls. Ever since she can remember, Nancy dreamed of one day going to Africa. She was intensely curious about the land, the tribes, the animals and the culture. In 1987, she experienced Africa for the first time and her reverence for it only deepened. Nancy would return again and again to quench her thirst.

On one of her trips, while looking for children to paint, Nancy discovered a small hut with 60 children in an impoverished fishing community. Nancy was amazed at these children who had lost parents and friends to AIDS, accidents and other illnesses. And many of these children had AIDS themselves. They had been facing death from the moment they were born. Nancy observed, "As has always been my experience in Africa, the children were full of enthusiasm despite their circumstances. No matter how much they lacked, they were still vibrant with laughter and kindness." After Nancy left the children that day, she promised to take care of them.

Thirteen years later, Nancy's preschool has 250 children and continues to grow. A new building was completed in 2011, and the children now have several teachers, access to supplies, a food program and a doctor on staff. The kids appropriately call Nancy "Mum," as she has mothered them all with her unwavering commitment.

Mrs. Tom

Matron, The N.A. Noël Preschool

Mrs. Tom started a small school for orphaned children in the Rusinga Island area of Kenya. Her experiences as a child (which included abuse and abandonment, hunger and homelessness), were the catalysts for her to help needy children.

Mrs. Tom realized that there were many children in her area who couldn't go to school because they couldn't pay the school fees, so she started a free school for those children. Thanks to the support and assistance of artist Nancy Noël, the school has grown to over 200 children.

The N.A. Noël Preschool has uplifted the entire community. Many of the children have been orphaned by the AIDS pandemic and are also infected with HIV/AIDS. The school is a place of safety where the children gather each day in hope, laughter and great joy, so they can flourish.

The Women Like Us Foundation helps support the school through donations and volunteers.

Mrs. Tom lives on the grounds with her extended family and watches over the school, the students and the teachers each day.

Mara Margaret Nyabuto

Tenderfeet Education Center

Mama Margaret Nyabuto is a courageous woman who has spent over 20 years serving the children in the slums of Kibera. In a response to the devastating effects of HIV/AIDS and poverty, Margaret formed the Tenderfeet Education Center in 2000.

A most remarkable woman, small in stature but big in heart, she has worked tirelessly to improve the lives of so many children and has paved the way for them to create fulfilling lives with a good education and a strong sense of self-worth.

Struggling by herself to keep the children together in the Center, she has faced tremendous setbacks and obstacles, including forced eviction, financial struggles, threats to her life and her school during riots, and dealing with the murder of her father in 2007.

None of these challenges breaks her resolve to create a sanctuary, a safe place of learning, for as many children as she can.

Margaret is convinced that long-term holistic projects that care for the emotional, physical, and spiritual needs of the residents—especially the children—are the best hope for the slums.

In 1991 she started teaching at a school in Kibera where she saw firsthand the widespread problem of the poorest children being unable to attend pre-primary and primary schools. After teaching throughout the 90s, she opened her own school in the year 2000. She called the new school Tenderfeet.

Her vision for Tenderfeet always was to reach the most vulnerable children in the slums. These are the orphans, victims of HIV/AIDS, children of prisoners, and those who faced a bleak future.

Ann Kabui

Founder of Victorious Teens Bridge International

Ann Kabui is a mother of one girl, and she is a friend to many vulnerable teenagers, providing them nurturing and support.

Ann worked in finances—specializing in marketing. She holds a diploma in business management from Kenya Institute of Management, and a diploma in Psychology. Ann participated in the formulation and amendment of the child policy act in Kenya, which took place in 2012 in Nairobi. She has always been passionate about working with children, and has won several awards for her commitment to leading programs for children in Kenya.

She is the founder and Executive Director at Victorious Teens Bridge International, a nonprofit organization located in East Africa, Nakuru (operating in Kenya) that supports teenagers in need in marginalized areas through guidance, counseling and providing supplies and equipment. Ann believes in nurturing gifts and talents using youth participatory approaches.

Ann is also a consultant in community programs that have assisted many local CBOs and youth groups that work with vulnerable children. She believes in the use of technology, especially when working with teenagers. Her Facebook account has been an online community for many teenagers who interact and engage with her on adolescent questions.

Currently, Ann is writing a magazine that targets both primary and secondary schools in Kenya on youth and reproductive health rights. Her vision is to see a future where every Kenyan youth is healthy, empowered and independent. In addition, she is working on a program "Beyond Classroom," which will help the teenagers realize their talents. She hopes to one day open a Vocational Training Centre for teens.

Beth Mwangi

Community Coordinator

Beth Mwangi lives in rural Kenya near the Rift Valley. She is a part of Victorious Teens International and is a community coordinator who works with over 100 teens and moms to help educate them on health and hygiene and to provide guidance for micro-enterprises.

At the time of the writing of this book, Beth is seeking donations to go to school to become a dental hygienist. In her own words:

Being a community worker in marginalized areas in Kenya, I have come across a lot of children and adults suffering from dental issues.

These communities are very poor and cannot afford toothpaste and brushes. While growing up, we used soft sticks from trees as toothbrushes but there was nothing to substitute for the paste.

I only realized my teeth had issues that could not be corrected, only removed, when I became an adult.

These same problems continue to face many children in marginalized areas and especially areas with high fluoride in the water. For instance, most adults in Central Rift Valley have brown teeth and end up removing them due to cavities.

With the knowledge of dental care, I would be able to help them and also educate them on simple, basic ways to maintain healthy teeth.

Kim DeWitt

Founder of Olmalaika Home

The Olmalaika Home in Sekenani, Kenya, is the result of God giving Kim DeWitt a heart and passion for young girls in Kenya who have no voice. It is also a result of her hard work and altruistic vision.

Kim is President of Global Village Ministries (GVM), a 501(c)(3) nonprofit based in the U.S. that provides medical and dental mission trips to Kenya three times each year. GVM also promotes long-term projects in the areas they visit, including building and education programs. The largest of these is The Olmalaika Home, which provides a safe home and education for young girls of the Maasai tribe who are at risk of female genital mutilation (FGM) and childhood marriage.

Kim's parents were missionaries, and she spent 12 of her first 14 years living in Kenya. In 2006, she began leading mission trips to Kenya, and was soon recruited by Norbert Schwer, then-President of GVM to be their Mission Trip Coordinator. It was not long after she began working with GVM that Norbert recognized her passion for the plight of the young Maasai girls, and he offered to support her in working with them.

There are currently 36 young girls living at Olmalaika, ranging in age from four to 20, with one getting her certificate in early childhood education and one in Teachers College. Each girl had a sponsor and the majority of the sponsors' cost covers schooling, uniforms, books, trips, transportation, school supplies, plus personal clothing and shoes.

Some of the girls are orphans; some are victims of FGM or childhood marriage, or have been rescued from that fate. Despite FGM being illegal in Kenya, it is still a real and frightening occurrence for many young Maasai girls. As Kim says, "Just ONE GIRL SAVED will impact the lives of many others. It is a ripple effect." Many of the girls have expressed the desire to become doctors, teachers, nurses or lawyers. The Olmalaika Home is changing lives and giving these girls incredible opportunities.

The home is dependent on people like you giving generously to make a difference. With that help, Kim's dream of saving these young girls becomes reality.

BIBLIOGRAPHY

Ali, Ayaan Hirsi. *Infidel.* New York: Atria. 2007.

Adichie, Chimamanda Ngozi. "The Danger of a Single Story." http://www.ted.com/talks/chimamanda_adichie_the_danger_of_a_single_story. Ted Global. 2009. www.Ted.com. 2016.

Angelou, Maya. *Phenomenal Woman: Four Poems Celebrating Women.* New York: Random House. January 17, 1995.

Barnett, Caroline. "Chapter Two. What's Your Trigger?" *Willing to Walk on Water: Step Out in Faith and Let God Work Miracles in Your Life.* Tyndale. 2013.

Breathnach, Sarah Ban. *Something More: Excavating Your Authentic Self.* New York: Warner Brothers, Inc. 1998.

Brehony, Kathleen A. *Living a Connected Life: Creating and Maintaining Relationships that Last.* New York: Henry Holt and Company. 2003.

Brown, Brene. *Daring Greatly.* New York: Avery. 2012.

Chatterjee, Siddharth. "Female Genital Mutilation in Kenya—When Will It End?" Huffington Post. November 25, 2014.

Chebii, Stella. "Menstruation and Education: How a Lack of Sanitary Towels Reduces School Attendance in Kenyan Slums." http://www.osisa.org/buwa/regional/menstruation-and-education-how-lack-sanitary-towels-reduces-school-attendance-kenyan-s. Open Society Initiative for Southern Africa. October 4, 2012. www.osisa.org.

Emmons, Robin. "Sowing Good in Community and Yourself." http://tedxcharlotte.com/2013/02/15/live-robin-emmons/. TedX Charlotte. March 21, 2013. www.Ted.com. August 2014.

"Fact Sheet: Youth Homelessness." http://www.endhomelessness.org/pages/youth_overview National Alliance to End Homelessness. January 19, 2010. www.endhomelessness.org.

K.D. Roche. http://freetobemedmst.com.

Hoen, Tory. "Ampersand Woman: CEO Alexandra Lebenthal." www.mmlafleur.com/ondash. MM.LAFLEUR. www.mmlafleur.com.

"Human Trafficking. A Global Problem." www.ice.gov./human trafficking. U.S. Immigration and Customs Enforcement. www.ice.gov. June, 2016.

Jordheim, Alisa. "Chapter Four: Familial Trafficking." *Made in the U.S.A.: The Sex Trafficking of America's Children.* Oviedo, FL.: HigherLife. 2014.

Kates, Erica. "More than Survival: Access to Higher Education for Low Income Women." http://www.centerwomenpolicy.org/programs/poverty/ Center for Women Policy Studies. www.centerwomenpolicy.org. 1991. Print.

Kazem, Halina. "Single moms often forgotten in San Francisco's homeless crisis." https://www.theguardian.com/society/2015/dec/18/san-francisco-homeless-crisis-single-moms-kids. *The Guardian.* December 18, 2015. www.theguardian.com.

Kristof, Nicholas D., Sheryl WuDunn. *Half the Sky: Turning Oppression into Opportunity for Women Worldwide.* New York: Alfred A. Knopf. 2009.

LaMarche, Pat. Pages 32 and 33. *Left Out in America: The State of Homelessness in the United States.* Portland, Maine: Upala Press. 2012. Print.

Leach, Monte. "A roof is not enough: A look at homelessness worldwide." www.shareinternational.org/archives/homelessness. Share International. October 15, 2005. www.shareinternational.org.

Lohmann, Raychelle Cassada MS, LPC. "Homeless Teens." *Psychology Today.* January 9, 2011. www.psychologytoday.com.

Molloy, Aimee. *However Long the Night: Molly Melching's Journey to Help Millions of African Women and Girls Triumph.* New York: Harper One. 2013.

Ntaiya, Kakenya. "A Girl Who Demanded School." http://www.ted.com/talks/kakenya_ntaiya_a_girl_who_demanded_school. TedX MidAtlantic. October 2012. www.Ted.com. June 2016.

O'Reilly, Nancy D. "Information: The Best form of Philanthropy" by Shirley Osborne. *Leading Women: 20 Influential Women Share Their Secrets to Leadership, Business and Life.* Avon, MA.: Adams Media. 2015.

Pacific Alliance to Stop Slavery. www.passhawaii.org.

Radcliffe, Shawn. "Meet the New Face of Homelessness: Children and Teens." http://americanspcc.org/meet-new-face-homelessness-children-teens/. Health Line. December 11, 2014. www.healthline.com.

Rubenstein, Michael. "Horrific Taboo: Female Circumcision on the Rise in U.S. NBC News. http://www.nbcnews.com/news/world/horrific-taboo-female-circumcision-rise-u-s-n66226. March 30, 2014. www.NBCNews.com. May 2016.

Sandberg, Sheryl. Page 19. *Lean In. Women, Work and the Will to Lead.* New York: Alfred A. Knopf. 2013.

Shared Hope International. www.sharedhope.org.

Sippel, Serra. "Saving Girls: Kakenya Ntaiya Is a CNN Hero." http://www.huffingtonpost.com/serra-sippel/kakenya-ntaiya-cnn-hero_b_4158928.html. *Huffington Post*. January 23, 2014. www.huffingtonpost.com.

Stone, Jan. "The Secret." "The Snowfall." *Absence of Tears: A Collection of True Stories of Homeless Women and Children*. Timothy Stone. 2015.

Teach for America. www.teachforamerica.org.

The Girl Effect. www.girleffect.org.

"U.S. Protect Women and Girls from Female Genital Mutilation (FGM)." http://www.equalitynow.org/action-alerts/protect-women-and-girls-female-genital-mutilation ww.Equality Now.org.

Wasserman, Jason Adam, Jeffrey Michael Clair. *At Home on the Street. People, Poverty and a Hidden Culture of Homelessness*. Boulder, CO: Lynne Rienner Publishers. 2010.

"Why Ida Odinga Is Not Your Average Politician's Wife." http://www.cnn.com/2012/05/28/world/africa/ida-odinga-kenya-prime-minister/index.html. CNN. June 22, 2012. www.cnn.com. July 2016.

Yousafzai, Malala. *I Am Malala: The Girl Who Stood Up for Education and Was Shot by the Taliban*. Great Britain: Phoenix Press. 2013.

BIBLIOGRAPHY

Linda Rendleman

Linda Rendleman is an award-winning writer, speaker and founder of the Women Like Us Foundation. Her previous books are a part of the Women Like Us Book Series and include *Women Like Us: Real Stories and Strategies for Living Your Best Life*; *Women Like Us: Illuminating the World*, and the current book, *Women Like Us: Together Changing the World* which is the inspiration for the upcoming documentary *Women Like Us. Three Journeys. One Mission. To Change the World.* of which she is also the Executive Producer.

She is a longtime champion of women, activist and humanitarian. Her travels around the world have included humanitarian work in Africa, India, Costa Rica, the Dominican Republic and the United States.

She has won numerous awards for her speaking and writing to women, including the Torchbearer Award from the State of Indiana, the highest award the state gives a woman, for her work supporting women's work, writing, and speaking. In the past, she has directed and produced her own television show on the Fox Network and her own radio show on local station WXNT in Indianapolis, Indiana.